LIVING
WITH JOY

BOOK I • EARTH LIFE SERIES

LIVING WITH JOY

Keys to Personal Power & Spiritual Transformation

25th Anniversary Edition

An Orin Book by

Sanaya Roman

H J Kramer

published in a joint venture with

New World Library
Novato, California

An H J Kramer Book
published in a joint venture with
New World Library

Editorial office:
H J Kramer Inc.
PO Box 1082
Tiburon, California 94920

Administrative office:
New World Library
14 Pamaron Way
Novato, California 94949

Library of Congress Cataloging-in-Publication Data
Orin (Spirit)
 Living with joy : keys to personal power and spiritual transformation : an Orin book / by Sanaya Roman. — 25th anniversary ed.
    p.   cm. — (Earth life series ; bk. 1)
 ISBN 978-1-932073-51-5 (pbk. : alk. paper)
 1. Spirit writings. 2. Self-realization—Miscellanea. 3. Telepathy. I. Roman, Sanaya. II. Title.
 BF1301.O72 2011
 133.9'3—dc22   2011009271

First printing, June 2011
ISBN 978-1-932073-51-5
Printed in the USA on 100% postconsumer-waste recycled paper

 New World Library is a proud member of the Green Press Initiative.

10 9 8 7 6 5 4 3

*To all of you who are learning to grow through joy
rather than through struggle or pain, for opening the door
for humanity to do the same.*

Contents

NOTE FROM SANAYA ABOUT THE COVER ART: *FLOWER LIGHT* BY HAL KRAMER (1914–2008)

Hal called me one day a number of years ago, saying he had received the inner guidance to print Orin's *Living with Joy* book. He and Linda Kramer had read the original *Living with Joy* manuscript, which had found its way to them. At that time, Hal thought he had retired from publishing, having sold his very successful publishing company, Celestial Arts. He did not plan on starting another publishing company, but when he saw the manuscript of *Living with Joy*, he felt impelled to publish it because he believed in the message of the book and felt it would help many people. The day before the deadline of printing *Living with Joy*, with no cover art yet, Hal wandered into an exhibition of Judith Cornell's lovely paintings, and he knew right then that he had found a cover for the *Living with Joy* book.

Now, years later, Hal is providing us with the cover art for this twenty-fifth anniversary edition of *Living with Joy*. At the young age of seventy-nine, Hal decided to take up a new career in painting, and he became an accomplished artist. Many of his acrylic paintings are featured in full color in his book, *Moments of Union: The Spiritual Paintings of Hal Kramer*. Hal's paintings bring to life the joy and higher energies that he was aware of and was able to capture in his artistic work. I have always enjoyed looking at Hal's paintings in his book, so when it came time to issue the anniversary edition of this book, I knew one of his paintings would be just perfect for the cover of this book. I found it in the *Flower Light* painting.

Even though Hal is no longer with us on the earth plane, his spirit lives on through his beautiful artwork, all the books he has published, and the light he has brought to the world through his support of and belief in the work of others. I am deeply grateful to Hal and Linda Kramer for their part in bringing Orin's work to the world through publishing his books.

Welcome to the Anniversary Edition of Living with Joy

Welcome to this revised, updated edition of *Living with Joy*. Since I first wrote this book, hundreds of thousands of people have used and practiced the principles it contains.

This anniversary edition contains much new material, as well as all the original chapters to assist you in growing through joy, peace, and love, and releasing struggle and pain. The chapters and the Playsheets in the original book contain key concepts and processes for living with joy, and as such all the original information is included in this book. Furthermore, I have made a number of additions to the text to deepen and expand upon the principles taught in the original book edition. I have also added a Daily Joy Practice and a number of Joy Affirmations at the end of each chapter to aid you in bringing to life the understanding you are gaining as you read this book about how to live a more joyful, fulfilling life.

The more you study this book and work with the practices, the more you can get out of it, the more alive and self-assured you can feel, and the more expansion and growth you can experience. You can feel uplifted, able to handle confidently the people and situations in your life. You can sustain a feeling of inner peace no matter what is happening around you. You can love and enjoy your life. You can look forward to each day. You can learn how not to be negatively affected by other people's energy or by world events, but instead have a positive outlook and offer your positive energy to others as well. You can attract to yourself better circumstances through your positive outlook. You can live with joy!

How to Get the Most out of the Daily Joy Practices

In this revised edition, I have included a Daily Joy Practice at the end of each chapter. You can use these practices to accelerate and expand your ability to live with joy and to positively affect the world around you. You can work with the Daily Joy Practices over and over to assist you in aligning with your true, innermost self and experiencing its joy, peace, love, harmony, freedom, clarity, and much more on an ongoing basis.

At the beginning of each day (or whenever you choose), you can use the Daily Joy Practice to connect with your innermost self, receiving the wonderful qualities of its energy. You can experience each day in new and higher ways as you open to receive all the energy that your innermost self — your higher self and soul — has to offer you. Connecting with your innermost self allows you to bring your outer life into alignment with who you are deep within. You can then experience and express your true self throughout the day in your words, thoughts, feelings, and interactions with others.

The Daily Joy Practices ask you to picture the day ahead. You will imagine how your day might be as you bring to it some quality taught in the chapter, such as joy, self-love, opening to receive, inner peace, clarity, freedom, and reframing the negative into the positive.

It is most important to make contact with your innermost being.

The most important step in each practice is to make contact with your soul, your innermost self. As you do these practices, take time to feel this self and to believe that it is real, whether or not you can sense it, feel it, or visualize it. If you cannot sense your soul or innermost self in any particular way, *pretend* that it is with you, for it always is. Follow my suggestions to open to its love, light, harmony, joy, and peace as indicated in each practice.

Every time you make contact with your innermost self through your intention to do so, you are creating a bigger channel to this self. The more attention you put on this innermost self, the more it will be present in your life and the more its wonderful qualities will become a part of your consciousness.

As you make contact with your innermost self, its energy goes out ahead of you.

As you consciously connect with your soul, your innermost self, and visualize or imagine the day ahead, its energy goes out ahead of you. It clears obstacles and opens the way for you to have a higher, better, more positive day. Your soul provides you with many opportunities to experience whatever quality you are practicing that day. Know that whatever comes to you during the day will be because of your request to deepen a soul quality such as inner peace, joy, love, freedom, or clarity. Imagine that the Universe is arranging itself just for you to give you the gifts of consciousness you have asked for. Know that your true, innermost self is *always* working for you and with you, and it always has your highest good in mind.

You will be using your imagination to picture the day ahead. Your imagination is a powerful faculty, for as you connect with your innermost self and imagine living your day with a new quality, you are creating this as your reality. If you want, you can record these practices in your own voice and play them back to use as a daily meditation. In addition, I have provided audio recordings of these practices for you to use; for information about these, see the back of the book.

It is useful before bed, or sometime near the end of the day, to reflect on the events of the day and how you demonstrated the quality you focused on. Acknowledge whatever seemed new or different about your day. Note what opportunities presented themselves for you to experience the quality you focused on. Reflect on how it felt to respond in new ways, to hold different perspectives, thoughts, and feelings about yourself and others.

You can expand the practices in any way you want. As you deepen and open the connection to your innermost self, it may make you aware of other soul qualities to work on during the day besides those things I guide you to focus on in the practices. Your innermost self is very creative and loves to provide you with various means and methods to expand your capacity to live a joyful, harmonious, and peaceful life.

Stop and affirm your intention to work with your innermost self to produce concrete and positive changes in your life. Ask it to join you right now and to be present as you read this book. Be open to all the wonderful shifts in consciousness that lie ahead!

Instructions for the
Living with Joy Affirmations

I have created many *Living with Joy* Affirmations for you to use as a way to create as your reality the new thoughts and possibilities for living with joy offered in each chapter. You can use these affirmations as a way to experience even more deeply the transformation of consciousness that is possible as you read and use these principles. These affirmations highlight some of the key points, major concepts, and understandings provided in each chapter.

Affirmations are living energy,
bringing you gifts of consciousness.

Affirmations become living energy when practiced with conviction and feeling, with a sense of your connection to your innermost self. Each affirmation carries within it the seed of a completely new consciousness. Even saying it one time brings to you a seed of new consciousness. As you practice using affirmations, you can receive the many gifts that lie within each one of them. This new consciousness will unfold to the degree that the affirmation resonates with you, the strength of your intention to make it your reality, and your opening to receive it. Even if your inner guidance is to work with just one of the affirmations, any one affirmation can open up an entire universe of new perceptions and awareness.

You have the power to make these
affirmations your reality.

I designed the Joy Affirmations to trigger an awakening of your potential for more joy, freedom, and love as you use them. Thinking of these affirmations, pondering on what they mean for you, and then saying them silently or aloud to yourself can create a definite shift in your capacity for joy.

As you say these affirmations, pause and feel the reality and power of the "I" within you, your innermost self, to create these affirmations as your reality. The words themselves do not have power. It is the energy of your innermost self you are calling upon when you say these affirmations that has the power to make these thoughts a reality. Imagine feeling the power, love, and wisdom of the innermost part of your being, your soul and spirit, as you say each affirmation, strengthening your ability to make the affirmation come true for you. Use these affirmations as a way to open the doorway to all the riches and gifts of consciousness your true, innermost self is waiting to give you when you ask and are open to receive.

As you say these affirmations, make them a statement of your intention for these to become your reality. What does this mean? When you set your intention to have something, the Universe responds by assisting you in making your intention a reality. As you state these affirmations, imagine that you *intend* to have them as the reality you experience. Imagine that they are already your truth, not something you will have in the future, but something you have right now.

To make these affirmations into your reality, repeat them with feeling and understanding.

As you say each affirmation, bring all of your awareness to what you are saying. As you say them to yourself with feeling, you may find that new images, thoughts, understandings, and intentions are being formed in your mind. It is better to pick a few affirmations to work with that have meaning for you than to rotely go through the list. Affirmations will not assist you in creating a new reality if you repeat them mindlessly over and over. Instead, say each one with feeling. Open to the deeper meaning within the affirmation and the higher path it puts you on as this statement becomes your reality.

Repeat whatever affirmations appeal to you throughout the day until you can sense a shift, or feel that these statements are becoming something that is possible to have. There is much power in repetition. As you repeat these affirmations to yourself, the thoughts contained within them will settle into your consciousness and become a part of your reality. As this happens, your life will begin to change to match this new inner reality.

Practice reading these affirmations at different times of the day and in various states of consciousness. In the morning, pick out several you want to focus on, and repeat them throughout the day as you think of them. You can also find other affirmations you want to create as your reality, and ponder on them before you go to bed. Take those affirmations that have special meaning for you and write them out on a card, sheet of paper, or put them on your computer where you will view them often. You may also want to record these in your own voice, and play them back while you are working around the house, exercising, driving, or whenever you can listen to them.

Each affirmation can open a door
into a new way of thinking and living.

You may find that each time you return to the list of affirmations at the end of each chapter, you feel drawn to different affirmations than the last time you reviewed them. Certain affirmations that you did not notice before may catch your attention. Use only those affirmations that feel appropriate to you and are something you want to create as your reality. It is important that the words feel comfortable to you and aligned with who you are. Feel free to substitute other words that have a special meaning to you, for the power of affirmations increases when the statements feel comfortable and meaningful. You can make up your own affirmations as well.

*The affirmations provide a very potent
and powerful path to joy.*

You can use the affirmations in this book to accelerate the many wonderful and positive changes in your daily life that will come from putting into practice the principles and understandings taught in this book. Whether you read the chapters or do the practices, you can grow simply through practicing these affirmations, these statements of intention, and opening to receive the gifts of consciousness that are being held in each one. *[Note from Sanaya: We have an Affirmations Room on our website, www.orindaben.com, where you can read any number of free affirmations, including those in this book.]*

The Playsheets, Daily Joy Practices, and Joy Affirmations can be used together to greatly expand the shifts in your life and consciousness that are being offered in this book. They offer you many ways to practice living with joy, feeling the wonderful freedom, love, and peace of your innermost being.

Open to all that you can have and all that awaits you, for you can live with joy!

Introduction by
Sanaya Roman

I welcome all of you who are reading this book. If this is your first Orin book, I am delighted you are joining us in learning more about how to live with joy. If you have read other Orin books, I am glad to have this opportunity to join with you again as you take another step on your spiritual path as you open to more of the joy, peace, and love within you.

When Orin first suggested that we work on a twenty-fifth anniversary edition of *Living with Joy*, I immediately felt the joy that would come from being involved with this book on a day-to-day basis for an extended period of time. My publisher and friend, Linda Kramer, agreed that it was a good idea, so Orin and I started working on this revised *Living with Joy* book.

Since Orin's original version of *Living with Joy* had touched hundreds of thousands of people with its message of hope, love, and joy and created so many shifts in people's lives, Orin kept the original chapters and made a number of additions to the text to deepen and expand upon the principles taught in the original book edition. Orin also wanted to expand people's potential to live a joyful, loving, and peaceful life through adding a Daily Joy Practice and many new Joy Affirmations to the end of every chapter. The Daily Joy Practices offer many ways to experience the transformation that Orin offers in each chapter. The affirmations highlight the key shifts presented in each chapter. They are living seeds of consciousness that can unfold in your life as you say them to yourself while focusing on their meaning, in a state of open receptivity to the positive changes that these can bring about.

As I worked with Orin on the Daily Joy Practices and Joy Affirmations, as well as when I read and reread the information in each chapter and in the Playsheets, I experienced a shift in my feelings and ability to embody the principles and spiritual truths contained in this book. Even though I have studied and used these principles for many years, I began to recognize subtle ways in which I could lift my thoughts to a higher level and feel even more joyful, hopeful, and optimistic about my life, other people, and the world around me.

Living with Joy *can assist you in creating wonderful and positive changes in your life.*

This book, *Living with Joy*, was "given" to me by a non-physical guide, a source of wisdom I call Orin. I have been channeling Orin, a spiritual guide and teacher, for many years. I experience Orin as a loving, wise, and gentle master teacher, always positive and compassionate. I am conscious of Orin's guidance as it comes through me. When I connect with Orin, I feel a heightened sense of serenity, clarity, and wisdom, as well as an expansive love that fills my heart. Orin's words seem like a fraction of what I am experiencing; there is a richness of feeling, pictures, and illumination transmitted with his words that are beyond description.

I am in a relaxed yet alert state of awareness when I bring Orin's messages through me. I am fully aware of both my own thoughts and his. My voice does not change, nor do I lose consciousness. It is as if through Orin I can experience a world of increased understanding, expanded awareness, and a higher, clearer vision of all the potential that lies within each person. It is clear that Orin embodies love and that he has deep love for humanity.

People often ask who Orin is. Orin tells me he is a being of light, and he says that who he is is not important; what matters is the message he brings and how useful that message is to you. He wants the focus to be on you and your growth, not upon himself. He never tells people what to do or how to live their lives. When asked, Orin will offer suggestions and ideas to assist people in becoming aware of more choices. People have repeatedly found that following Orin's advice expands them, opens them to their innermost selves, and brings them joy. Orin and I encourage you to read this book for the wisdom it contains, not because of any claims made about its source.

Orin is always positive and encouraging. He has an enduring message: The Universe is friendly and always working for us (even if we cannot always see how this is true), the Universe is unlimited in its abundance, and we can grow through joy rather than through pain or struggle.

Orin originally taught the material in this book to a small group of students to teach them how to live with joy and stop growing through pain, struggle, or crisis. Orin told us that the information covered in the classes would be the basis for a book called *Living with Joy*. He said that he was aware of each of you who would be reading this book, for in his reality there is no time and space.

As you read this book, be aware that Orin is talking to you, and he was aware that you would be reading and working with the principles taught in this book. As Orin and I put this book together, both the original book and the anniversary edition, he often had me stop and allow him to broadcast energy to you who were connecting with and asking for his light and support. I sensed an enormous amount of love pouring through me during those times. Know that Orin's love and support, as well as that of your own innermost self, is always available when you ask for it and are open to receive.

At other times while we were working on this book, Orin had me send out love through my heart to all of you as a group. He had me imagine everyone reading this book as a loving, connected community of like-minded souls, assisting each other through this inner connection in strengthening our ability to live with joy and to let go of growing through pain and struggle. He says that all of us together are generating a group light that is becoming a profound source of awakening for others who are following, one step behind — those who are ready to also let go of pain and struggle and grow with joy instead.

Throughout his books and audio courses Orin always suggests that you connect with your innermost self, your soul and spirit, as he will guide you to do throughout *Living with Joy*. It is this self that creates all transformation and draws to you the perfect circumstances, relationships, and situations that allow you to expand and grow. In this book Orin uses the terms *soul, spirit, higher self,* and *innermost self* interchangeably. He invites you to use whatever term best describes the innermost part of your being as you read and work with all of the exercises in the book, including those in the Playsheets, Daily Joy Practices, and Joy Affirmations.

Orin reminds you to accept only the information that rings true to the deepest part of your being, your true, innermost self, and set aside any information that does not. He always tells people to follow their own wisdom and listen to the authority of their own soul above all else. Find within this book that which resonates with the truth in you.

Orin says he is working with us at this time because humanity is going through a major transition and awakening. Through his many books and audio courses, Orin is offering a path of spiritual awakening that we call *Orin's Path of Self-Realization*. *Living with Joy* is an important part of this path. In Orin's *Living with Joy* book, you will connect with your innermost self, your soul, to live a more joyful, positive, and loving life. With this connection, you will discover how to experience more of the joy, freedom, and love of your true, innermost self. You will learn how to have more inner peace, clarity, balance, self-respect, self-esteem, and self-love; to open to receive; to listen to the wisdom of your heart; to transform your subpersonalities; to change negatives into positives; to refine your ego; and to start recognizing and living your higher purpose.

With this book, I invite you to lift up your spirit and join with me in choosing joy, releasing struggle, and opening to your unlimited potential for personal power and spiritual transformation.

Learning to Channel

If you are interested in connecting with and channeling a guide yourself, it is possible to learn how to do so. Orin has taught thousands of people to channel through the *Opening to*

Channel book and audio courses on channeling that you may use if you feel drawn to meet and channel a guide yourself. To meet and channel a guide, you will need to have a sincere interest in working with a guide and be open to experiencing states of consciousness where you feel clearer, wiser, and more loving and inspired than usual. Channeling involves listening within and allowing yourself to expand beyond the "you" that you know as your normal awareness. It requires that you let your identity grow into one that includes a more expansive perspective. Channeling is a skill that you can learn, and Orin's *Opening to Channel* book will assist you in doing so.

Suggestions on How to Use This Book

People have shared with me throughout the years numerous ways they have found to use this book, and I want to share some of their suggestions that may enhance your own reading experience. What you may discover is that there are as many ways to read the book as there are readers, so choose what works best for you.

Many people found great value in reading this book straight through, chapter by chapter, including working with the Playsheets in the order given. Some people shared that they enjoyed reading the chapters straight through to absorb the positive information in them, then returned later to work with whatever Playsheets they were drawn to as a way to expand their ability to live the principles taught in the book.

Some people wrote that they took the book with them everywhere, referring to it throughout the day to help them handle their daily lives in higher ways. Often people talked about putting it by their bed, so they could read a chapter or several pages before bed. One woman shared, "Your book *Living with Joy* has been on my bedside for twenty years. I read it almost every day. It's been great guidance for me." Other people liked to read a little at the beginning of the day, finding it an uplifting way to start their day on a positive note. The Daily Joy Practices provide a wonderful way to do this.

Some people read a little of the book, put it down, then picked it up later and realized it was just what they needed. It is fine if you only read one chapter or use one practice; whenever you are ready for more, your innermost self will guide you back to this book. We heard from many people who started the book, and then years later picked it up again, reading it all the way through. They said they could not put it down until they were finished. As one man wrote, "I bought *Living with Joy* but only read a little of it. I was drawn back to the book recently. I am reading it now. I know why I had to wait to read it: I was not ready! It is an incredible book!"

Open this book to any page for a message.

Many people have loved the fact that they can open the book to any page and read it for the message it contains, which always seems helpful and relevant to whatever question they are asking or situation they are facing. One man wrote, reflecting on his experiences, "I am amazed at how consistently *Living with Joy* addresses the challenges at hand, especially when I open it to a random page. I read it a few years ago, and it was perfect for me then. I am reading it again now, and it applies even more now, and on a completely different level. As a channel myself, the book inspires me to rely more and more on my own guidance, and more often."

One woman shared with me in her note, "I will randomly open a page at night before I go to sleep and the right chapter always seems to appear with the message I need to hear and learn. It has calmed my spirit when I needed calming." Another man wrote, "When I am feeling low, my intuition will guide me to open the book, and no matter which page I open, it is always exactly what I need at that moment."

Because so many people have found value in random quotes from this book, we have created a special free webpage on our www.orindaben.com website called the Creating Your Highest Future Room, where you can click on the picture of this book, and random quotes from the book will appear for you to ponder and use.

Orin's teachings contain many layers and levels of information that can unfold more deeply with each reading.

Many people have found value in reading this book not only once but over and over again. You may find that reading the book or your favorite chapters again, or on an ongoing basis, will strengthen your ability to experience more joy, love, and peace. There is great wisdom behind Orin's words that can awaken your own wisdom as you read this book. Each time you study this book you can experience more insights, almost as if veils are being lifted and you are reading new material each time.

As one woman gratefully wrote, "*Living with Joy* is still an almost daily read for me, each page filled with such wonderful guidance and wisdom — a true gem, one of the best in my library. Every time I read *Living with Joy*, I gain something new from it, so it never feels like I am reading the same thing again at all. It always answers my questions and doubts in a beautiful, loving way."

Read and share this book with other people.

You may enjoy reading and sharing this book with other people. I have heard from a number of people about the joy they received in reading and working with the principles, truths, and exercises in this book with someone else. They found that it was fun and brought them many benefits to work on the book with others. As one woman shared, "*Living with Joy* resonated with all my deepest personal feelings about life. It is so easy to get caught up in all the trivial distractions in life. Whenever I would read *Living with Joy*, I would again feel aligned with my truth. I began to read a chapter a day with my husband, and we would do the Playsheets together, and we both enjoyed that time together. It has greatly improved our relationship."

I received many notes from people letting me know of all the people with whom they had shared the *Living with Joy* book. They said they have found this book so practical and useful, and experienced such a positive change in their feelings and outlook on the world, that they gave copies of the book to everyone they knew. I heard from people things such as, "I have recommended and given your books to almost everyone I know. They are especially comforting and empowering when people are in crisis."

Teach the principles in this book to others.

Many people have written to us letting us know that they were teaching this book as a class to other people. They let me know of their class dates, gave me their students' names, and Orin and I transmitted light to the teachers and to all their students. There is additional information on our website about offering this and our other books as classes.

The principles in this book are timeless.

As one woman wrote, "I've loved reading *Living with Joy*. I'm amazed that the books read so fresh and contemporary even though they were written many years ago. The information in these books is timeless."

The spiritual truths taught in this book are indeed time-less and have been taught by many spiritual teachers throughout the centuries. In the written material, the Playsheets, Daily Joy Practices, and Joy Affirmations, Orin teaches you practical ways to understand and use spiritual principles and truths to live a more fulfilling life. These truths are as true now as they were in the past and will be in the future, for spiritual truths will always be applicable, no matter when you study them.

Stories from Our Readers

Over the years, people have written that the information in Orin's *Living with Joy* book touched them deeply; in fact, for many the book was given to them or recommended to them by someone who thought it would make a difference in their lives. They felt that *Living with Joy* offered them many prac-tical and uplifting ideas, in an easy to understand way, which they could immediately use to change their lives for the better.

People have written to me with many wonderful stories of the many ways the book has helped them. I love hearing from you about your experiences, as you are the reason Orin is here. Orin wrote these books for you. Your stories have touched my heart and showed me the depth of how much you are ready and willing to change your life for the better, once you find effective ways to do so. It is my hope that sharing a few people's stories will assist you in recognizing some of the potential ways your life can change for the better as you work with the principles and practices offered in this book. We have included more stories from our readers in the back of this book, beginning on page 227.

— Sanaya Roman

CHAPTER ONE

Greetings from Orin

Greetings from Orin to you who are here to learn about the higher levels of wisdom. Once you master these levels, daily living becomes simpler, and the challenge then becomes one of reaching even higher levels and staying there. I am taking all of you there so that you may pass on the information, for you who are apprentices now will be the teachers later, having your own students in time. These students will be anyone who will benefit from your love and wisdom, including your family and friends. The wiser and more compassionate you become, the more others will naturally seek out your counsel and advice. I speak to you to assist you in reaching a new, more expanded state of awareness and being that will enable you to be leaders, teachers, and healers.

I am offering you an opportunity to be among those who are moving into expanded levels of consciousness and awareness of how to live with joy and to release pain and struggle. For this wisdom, once you read and assimilate it, will seem as if you have known it all along. Anything you learn you may find yourself giving to others, as well as using for your own understanding and guidance. I am calling to any of you who are here as teachers and healers, even if you are not yet aware of who you are, to step out of the common mass thinking, to go beyond your known reality and enter into higher realms of light and love.

I will assist you in reaching your soul and its greater awareness, helping you discover the joy that awaits as you look through the windows of your soul. Joy is an attitude; it is the presence of love — for self and others. It comes from a feeling of inner peace, the ability to give and receive, and appreciation of yourself and others. It is a state of gratitude and compassion, a feeling of connection to your innermost self, your soul.

In this book, you will learn how to create a nurturing, supportive environment in which your spirit, your true, innermost self, can unfold. I will help you recognize your path and higher purpose and show you how to open to it. I have dedicated this book to helping you see who you really are, to showing you how to step onto the path of joy and light. The information, suggestions, processes, practices, and affirmations it contains can enable you to live a life of ease, and yet I smile lovingly as I say *ease*. For those situations you consider difficult right now you will soon handle with grace, but wonderful new challenges will come, which you will also learn to handle with grace and ease.

You experience many states of awareness that you often do not pay attention to. You can learn to become aware of higher levels of information and consciousness by focusing on them. You can experience knowledge and true wisdom. I will assist you in exploring and expanding your ability to listen to your soul's guidance. You will learn to tap into whatever information the Universe has that will assist you.

Each of you who feels called to this book can be a channel of healing and love. Each of you is on the path of planetary service and accelerated personal evolution. You express it in many different ways, such as healing through your hands, sharing wisdom through speaking, writing, or assisting others, and spreading light and love to those around you.

Many realities exist, and I would like to lead you into some of the higher and finer realms of love, joy, and wisdom. I ask you, as you read this, to reach out and stretch your thinking into new ideas that right now the masses may not accept. As human consciousness expands, more and more people will reach these new levels of love and wisdom. These concepts will be the norm one hundred years from now.

*You are seeding the world
with new thoughtforms.*

I extend an invitation to anyone who is willing to participate in the opportunities that are coming and in the opportunities that are already here. Imagine yourself as part of a larger group, all coming together to explore consciousness, to seed the Universe with new ideas. These are beliefs that the Universe is friendly, that it is abundant, and that you can live in a state of joy and love. As you contribute your higher thoughts to the "general atmosphere," you create ideas that will assist others in loving themselves more.

I am inviting those of you on a path of light and joy to join with my essence as you read these pages and feel the community of all who are sharing this knowledge and wisdom. A group of people, holding certain thoughtforms in their joint mind, can accomplish much. Whenever certain thoughts and beliefs are held and practiced by a group of people — and the focus is love, spiritual growth, and higher purpose — they magnify tenfold the ability of each person to create them in his or her life and to make those thoughts available to others who are reaching upward.

The world is undergoing much spiritual transformation. Major changes are happening in the mass thoughtforms, and this will continue to happen for many hundreds of years. You can help plant the new thoughts that will lift and evolve humankind. You can hold an image of greatness, of universal concerns, and of helping the earth itself. To utilize the energy and opportunities during these and future times, you will need to develop such soul qualities as peace, clarity, love, and joy. I am not speaking of a worldwide calamity that is coming, for I do not see that happening. I am speaking of the need to bring peace to the planet by bringing peace into your own life. Take this opportunity to utilize the energy and transitional atmosphere of these times to propel yourself into a higher consciousness.

There are many wise teachers, and we are all bringing through the same message of universal love, peace, and oneness. We speak in different vocabularies, using the words that best reach the groups with whom we are communicating. It is happening in many places. You have probably felt a sense of community with all those who are focusing on expanded aware-ness and self-growth. You may find yourself in two worlds, connecting with people who do not believe in these things and those who do. You may discover that you have relationships that span several worlds, for this information must be planted in many places. We are encouraging people to cross-pollinate the world, to be a part of more than their own group of like-minded people, to be willing to reach out to people in other fields of work and study, with different interests. The more areas you can be a part of, the more valuable you and your ideas will be to the planet.

You can learn ways to transcend power struggles and move your relationships into the heart and soul, connecting with each other in a more loving way. As you read, you will explore many joyful ways to link with your friends and others in your life, to establish connections that will bring you joy and inner peace. You who read this are on a path of uniting with other people from the heart and not from the power center. You can pass on and share what you discover. It is time for new thoughtforms on the planet, new ways of joining and being with each other, ways that create peace and not disharmony.

Who am I?

So many of you have asked, what is a guide? Who are we? What is our purpose? I, Orin, am a spiritual teacher. I can exist in other systems of reality besides those based on your scientific principles and laws. I have experienced a lifetime on this planet so I could understand better the experience of physical reality.

I travel into many systems. In your world, you might call me a researcher, reporter, teacher, and guide, but that is only part of who I am. I connect with many planes of reality, for right now on an interplanetary scale there is great growth and evolution occurring in all kingdoms. In the worlds I travel to, growth is accelerating. Many beings of light, masters, enlightened ones, and the angels are here to help you if you ask.

I am a Being of Light.

I am assisting you who are on a path of light and joy on earth, who are willing to serve the planet through your interest in personal growth and evolution. I offer guidance and

assistance in both your personal life and your path of world
service.

I am transmitting spiritual teachings to the earth plane.
Certain truths operate throughout the known universes; I am
here to offer you those spiritual truths, principles, and practices that can assist you in living a more joyful, fulfilling life.
The understanding and practice of these truths always creates
expanded awareness and growth.

I invite your soul to join with me as we explore your greater
potential. My essence is behind the thoughts in this book and
will help you open to your deeper, wiser self. It will feel as
if you are becoming who you always knew you were. Many
of you have always felt different from those around you, as if
you knew you had a mission, something special to accomplish
with your life. I hope to help you discover more about that
mission and purpose. I invite you to journey with me to the
realms of light and love that you come from.

Many of you beautiful souls of light have gotten caught
in the denser energies of the earth. With the concepts in this
book, I will attempt to lead you back to those finer realms you
so naturally seek. Allow yourself to absorb the energy behind
the words, for I have written this book in such a way that both
the words and the energy I send with them will assist you in
opening your heart.

*There is great love,
compassion, and guidance
available through us,
the Beings of Light.*

I am not distant, and my love and guidance is available to any who ask for it. You must ask, however, before the Universe can give anything to you. I and others who offer assistance from the higher realms cannot help those who do not ask.

This is the beginning of the course. What I am saying is but a small part of what will be happening to all of you as you open to your innermost self and follow a path of joy. I hope that in some way I can make your transition to a higher consciousness more joyful, for all of you drawn to this book are undergoing major change and personal and spiritual transformation. I encourage you to accept into your heart only those ideas and suggestions in this book that ring true to the deepest part of your being, and let go of any that do not. I am here as an assistant and spiritual teacher, to aid you with your personal transformation. I welcome you to a more joyful, loving, and peaceful vision of who you are.

CHAPTER TWO

You Can Live Joyfully

I will speak of joy, compassion, and higher purpose, for many of you are searching for peace and a sense of inner completion. Most of you are aware that peace comes from your inner world and that the outer world is a symbolic representation of that which is within. You are all at different levels of perceiving the process by which you create what you experience.

What is the path of joy? There are many life-paths you can choose, just as there are many ways you can serve on a planetary level. There is a path of will, a path of struggle, and a path of joy and compassion.

> *Joy is an inner note*
> *that you sound*
> *as you move through*
> *the day.*

What brings joy into your life? Do you know? Are you aware of that which makes you happy? Are you so busy fulfilling your daily obligations that you put off to some future time those things that make you feel good? The path of joy deals with present and not future time. Are you holding an image of what life *will be* like one day when you are happy, but not feeling that sense of well-being right now, today?

Many of you fill your time with activities that are not soul-directed but with activities of the personality. People may have taught you that self-worth comes from being busy. There are two kinds of busyness, however. Personality-directed activities are often based on "shoulds" and do not express your higher purpose. Soul-directed activity is always an expression of your higher purpose.

The senses often distract the personality, capturing its attention from moment to moment. The phone call, the child, the constant voices, the emotions of others — all are energies that grab your attention throughout the day and can distract you from your inner-directed messages.

True joy comes from operating with
inner-directedness and recognizing
who you are.

You may have many reasons why you cannot change your life right now. If you do not create reasons why you can, change will always be a future thought, and you will not be on the path of joy. In this world you have chosen to come into, you have been given physical senses and an emotional body. Your great challenge is to not be distracted by that which happens in front of you, or is pulling on you or calling to you, but instead to find your center and magnetize to yourself all those things that are in alignment with your inner being.

Are you setting it up so that people are pulling on you, so that your time is full, but you are not filling it with the things you want? You have the power to change that drama. It comes from your compassion for who you are and from your sense of inner freedom.

Many of you have set up lives for yourselves that are not joyful because you believe that you are obligated to others or you are entrapped by your own need for other people to need your help.

The challenge of the path of joy is to create freedom.

Every person is free. You may have created an arena of work and based your life upon certain accomplishments and forms. The path of joy is learning how not to be caught by the details of those forms. It is learning how not to be trapped by your own creations, but to be uplifted by them.

If you have created a job, a relationship, or anything that is not bringing you joy, look inward and ask why you feel you must be in a relationship with anything or anyone that does not bring you joy. Often it is because you do not believe you deserve to have what you want. There is no such thing as "deserving" on our plane. You all have active imaginations; they are your doorways out of where you are. Yours can be a doorway into worry, if that is how you use it, or it can be a doorway into joy.

As you are on the phone during the day, speaking to your friends, do you let them talk on long past when you would like the conversation to be finished? Do you listen to their stories, even when those stories bring down your energy? Do you make appointments to see people, even though you do not truly have the time, or when there is no higher purpose in being with them? To find the path of joy you will want to ask why you feel obligated to people or to the forms you have created.

The path of compassion does not obligate you to love people regardless of how they act or who they are. It is a path of seeing the truth of who people are, acknowledging all their parts, their humanness as well as their divinity. It is the path of looking at people and asking, "Is there anything I can do to heal, assist, or bring them in touch with their higher vision?" If there is not, then you are pulling down your own energy by spending time with them.

Some of you help people over and over, feeling frustrated. You may feel obligated, as if there were no way out except to listen to their tales of woe, wishing that they would get on with their lives and change their circumstances. If you are helping people and they are not growing, then you had better look again to see if you are indeed helping them or if they are capable of receiving the help you are giving.

The path of joy involves the ability to receive. You can surround yourself with love, friends that care, and have a healthy and fit body, if you choose. There is so much to be grateful for and appreciate. One of the ways to receive more is to spend time appreciating what you have. Acknowledge even the simplest things — the flowers you see or smell, the heart-warming smile of a child, the food you eat — and you will soon find the Universe sending you even more good things, for gratitude is magnetic.

For those of you who are concerned about money or finding a career where you can make money doing what you love, have you been willing to take a risk and do what you love? Have you been willing to trust the Universe to give the oppor-tunity to you? And even more, are you prepared to handle the money when it comes? Do you feel you deserve it?

*The path of joy involves
valuing yourself and monitoring
where you put your time.*

If people spent time only where they accomplished the greatest good for themselves and the people they were with, the world would change in a day. It is important to spend time in ways that promote your highest good. If something is not for your highest good, I can guarantee that it is not for the highest good of the planet or other people either.

You may ask, "What am I here to do that will bring me joy?" Each one of you has things that you love to do. There is not one person alive who does not have something he or she loves to do.

*What you love is a sign from
your higher self of what
you are to do.*

You may say, "I love to read and meditate; certainly that cannot be my path and bring me money." However, if you allowed yourself to sit, read, and meditate, a path would unfold. So often you resist what you most want to do. In everyone's mind there is a whisper of the next step. It may be simple, such as making a phone call or reading a book. It may be a very concrete, mundane step to take that may not even seem connected with your higher vision. Know that you are always being shown the next step; it is always something that comes to your mind as an obvious, simple, and joyful thing to do.

You all know what would bring you joy tomorrow or someday in the future. When you wake up, ask yourself what you could do *today* that would bring you joy and delight. Put a smile on your face, rather than focusing on how you are going to get through another day. Do not focus on the problems you have to handle.

> *You will have joy only when*
> *you focus on having it and*
> *settle for nothing less.*

What is your highest vision, and how do you find it in your life? Most of you have many distractions that need not be. If you were to sit for even five minutes each day, or for one minute several times a day, reviewing what you set up for the day, and ask how each appointment, person, or phone call fits into your higher purpose, in a few short months you would be on the path of your destiny. Of course, you will need to *act* upon this wisdom to bring a new higher path into your life.

If you do not know what your path is, you can create a symbol for it. Imagine that you are holding it in your hands as a ball of light. Bring it up to your heart, then into your crown chakra at the top of your head, and release it to your soul. Very shortly, it will begin to take form. You will find that with just the thought of higher purpose you will begin to magically rearrange your day. Over time, friends who wasted your time will no longer seem interesting. You may bring new friends into your life and change the nature of your activities and connection with existing friends.

Compassion is caring for yourself — valuing yourself and your time. You do not owe anyone your time. When you take charge of yourself and affirm that you are a unique and valuable person, the world will affirm it to you also.

Every person has a purpose and a
reason for being on earth.

There is not just one thing you are here to do, for each thing you accomplish becomes part of an earlier step and another stage of your evolution. Each experience flows from earlier experiences. Some of you step sideways, trying out new and seemingly unrelated things, to bring in new skills on the journey upward. Some of you find form for your work. Do not judge purpose by the standards of others, or by what society has told you are the best things to do. You may be here to develop inner peace and radiate that quality outward, making it available to others. You may be here to explore the realm of the intellect or the business world, to assist the thoughtforms on the planet at that level. Compassion is outside of judgment. It is simple acceptance, the ability to love and to value yourself and whatever path of higher purpose unfolds.

There is tension worldwide at almost all times, but there is also great opportunity available for those who focus on the positive and are willing to take responsibility for everything they create. Energy is available to those who are intuitive and healing and on a path of joy. That energy brings you the opportunity to have great abundance and joy now.

Many of you are moving ahead rapidly. You have been on an accelerated path of growth so that you may heal and teach others who are following. Some of you, such as authors and writers, may be years ahead of the mass thoughtforms, as it is necessary for you to be in the flow of the times when you release your work to the world.

All of you reading this
are pioneers, for you would not be
attracted to this information
if you were not ahead of your time.

You may be feeling a change in the energy of the planet. Those of you who are willing to look upward and find your vision will find your lives even more accelerated. If you think you are busy right now — be prepared! Things will happen even faster, and that is why acting with wisdom and discernment is increasingly important. That is why you will want to look at each day and compare it to your higher purpose.

Sometimes the hardest thing of all is saying no to someone in need. If you constantly pay attention to people in crisis, you affirm that the way for them to get your attention is by creating crisis. If you want people in your life to respect and honor your time, teach them by rewarding them when they do so.

The world is going through a change; things are speeding up. You may already be feeling it. Those who do not focus on their higher vision and connect with their true, innermost self may experience even more problems. Some of the people around you may be speaking of this as the greatest, most joyful time of their lives, while others are speaking of it as one of the most difficult times. If you are experiencing this as the most joyful time in your life, look around at others. Rather than judging or feeling separate from those who are having difficulties, simply send them light, and then let go. Know that their soul and higher self is taking care of them, and that they are learning exactly the lessons they need to learn to evolve spiritually and become stronger and wiser.

If you find yourself in power struggles with people — strangers, loved ones, or close friends — connect with your higher self, the center of your being. Stop for a moment, take a deep breath, and do not get caught in their desire for a confrontation. Remember, it is their desire, *not* yours.

To live a joyful life, you will want to learn how to not let other people pull you into their negative energy through the third chakra, the solar plexus center. Much of the energy that people experience from others comes through the solar plexus, the power and emotional center. Many of your challenges on the path of joy will be to step outside of power struggles and come from a deep level of compassion. If a friend snaps at you or is unfriendly, step back, and with a sense of compassion, try to experience life from his or her perspective. You may see that his or her tiredness or defensiveness has nothing to do with you, for you only represent another character in his or her play. The more you can step outside and not be pulled into power struggles, the more peaceful and abundant your life will be, and the more you will be in a position to heal others by being in your heart with compassion.

Go inward for a moment and ask yourself what you can do today or tomorrow, specifically, to bring more joy into your life. Ask what you can do to let go of a power struggle or an issue that is going on in your life and draining your energy. What can you do today or tomorrow to free up a little more time so you can experience inner peace?

You have so much to be grateful for, your excellent mind and your unlimited potential. You have the ability to create anything you want; the only limits are those you create for yourself. Wake up in the morning and affirm your freedom. Hold up your higher vision and live the most joyful life you can imagine.

You Can Live Joyfully
PLAYSHEET

1. Think of seven things you love to do, that feel joyful when you do them, that you have not done in the last several months. They may be anything — lying in the sun, taking a trip, getting a massage, accomplishing a goal, exercising, reading a book.

2. As you think of these things, reflect on what stops you from doing each one — something either inside (such as your feelings) or outside (someone or something, such as lack of money, that keeps you from it).

3. Take two or three of the things that hold the most joy for you, and think of one step you can take toward each to bring it into your life.

4. Mark your calendar with a date and a time that you will bring each of these joyful activities into your life.

DAILY JOY PRACTICE

If you choose, decide that you will begin living joyfully, regardless of what is happening in your life or the world around you. To start living joyfully, pause for a moment, take a breath in, and connect with your innermost self, simply by having the intention to do so. It is fine if it feels like you are using your imagination or if the connection only lasts for a few seconds. Your true, innermost being is always with you. This is who you are deep within. This self is joyful!

Imagine that you are tapping into the joy that has always been within you. You have had many moments of joy in your life, and you are now deciding to create and experience more moments of joy. Ask your innermost self to flood your entire personality, your whole being, with its joy. As it does, open to receive and experience the joy that is your birthright; that is the essence of who you are.

Picture how you will feel as you allow yourself to experience joy throughout the day in everything you do and with all the people you encounter. Sense how your joyful energy lifts everyone around you. Your joy is a gift to the world; your joy brings joy to others. Imagine how you will feel at the end of the day or week as you allow yourself to live more joyfully.

AFFIRMATIONS

I choose to live joyfully.

I am willing to grow through joy
rather than through pain or struggle.

The joy of my innermost being shines through me.

I express the joy of my soul as I move through the day.

I am joyful right now.

I love feeling joyful, and I feel this way often.

I am loving and kind to myself.

My joy brings joy to others.

I am aware of my innermost being.
It guides and directs me.

I draw to myself circumstances, activities,
and people that are in alignment with my innermost being.

I am free.

I am willing to do those things that bring me joy.

I am free to be around joyful people, and I am!

I deserve to have a wonderful, joyful life of abundance,
good friends, and meaningful activities, and I do.

I am doing what brings me joy for a living.

I value my time and energy.

I am a unique and valuable person.

I stay in my center around other people.

I know who I am.
My vision of my potential and myself expands
every day.

I recognize and acknowledge all the
joyful moments in my life.

I am joyful.

CHAPTER THREE

Changing the Negative into the Positive

The ability to see all situations, people, and events from a positive perspective will help you rise out of the mass thoughtforms and the denser levels of energy and onto your path of joy. You can bring to the people around you the belief that everything happens for their good.

It is common to hear people complain, speak of being victims, or go on and on about the negative things that happen to them. Most speaking and communication — on TV, in private and public conversations — center around what is wrong and bad. Many people have developed a way of thinking and interacting with others that has strong overtones of righteousness, outrage, or right and wrong, and the emphasis is usually on what is wrong. This has at its root your system of polarities, where something is either good or bad, positive or negative, up or down. Changing negatives into positives is part of spreading the belief in higher good.

Because you exist in a system of polarities, I cannot speak in a meaningful way without using that framework, so I will use that system in communicating to you. You can educate those you come in contact with about the positive reasons why things are happening to them.

*If you wish to be aware of the higher
good happening in your own life,
be willing to let go of a limited
perspective and enlarge your
view of your life.*

In many ways your past acts as an anchor until you release and let go of any negative beliefs or memories about it. Some of you have past relationships you feel you did not handle in the best way you could. Maybe there is an old hurt in your heart, a feeling of being let down or of having let another person down. You can go back and change negative memories by looking at the gifts people offered you and seeing the good you did for them. You then can telepathically transmit forgiveness and love to those people at whatever age they were when you knew them. Forgive yourself and think kind thoughts of yourself. You will heal yourself and others by doing this. The healing will occur in the present time also, and this can stop you from projecting these negative patterns into your future.

I will start by speaking of the past, for many of you hold negative images about your past selves. Every day you are growing, evolving, and learning new ways to handle your energy, and yet, if it had not been for those incidents in the past, you would not be who you are now.

*Everything that happens is meant
to help move you into your greater self.*

Now that you have reached a new level of being, you may be tempted to look back at the past with regret. You may think of many higher, more loving ways you could have handled some issues and situations. Yet those very incidents provided you with the growth that allows you now to see a better way of behaving. Some lessons may be more painful than others, depending on how willing you are to face them. When I speak of enlarging your scope of vision, I am speaking of being able to step outside of the present and see your life as a whole rather than as a series of unconnected events.

When I, as Orin, view a person, I stand above his or her entire life. I see each incident not as a separate event but as a part of an entire life-path. You have the ability to do this also. You may resist it, or feel unwilling to take the time, and yet great gifts await you if you are willing to see your life from a larger perspective. To reframe the negative into the positive, the conscious mind needs to see the larger picture. Your innermost self already sees the larger picture. By learning to move into that larger perspective and out of the emotional and mental body, you can see your life more positively.

Many people's emotions are affected by worldwide belief systems that create fear and pessimism. It is our intent, through holding a constant focus of peace and love, to contribute optimism and hope to the emotional atmosphere and belief systems of people.

The newspapers and the mass media often communicate a feeling of doom that pervades the mental images and emotional feeling tones of a nation. Since I am reframing negatives into positives, I will add there are *good* reasons why this is happening. If you look at the world from a larger perspective, you will see that humanity is changing the path it is on in part because of these fear-based messages. People respond to certain kinds of messages, and most react to the negative ones being put out, including those that warn and that trigger fear. Right now, it seems that fear works more effectively to change people than hope; and yet, once the tide has turned, it will be time for new communications of hope and optimism.

When you look around at your society, become aware of the way people are speaking. Notice the ways they are learning about their energy. Broadcast to them your belief that they can grow with joy, in positive ways. There are some belief systems that are undergoing change. I will mention them so you may assist in bringing through the higher systems of reality more rapidly.

One is a belief that growth comes through pain and struggle, which is one you are getting ready to let go of on a mass level. However, many people are not yet ready to exist without pain and struggle, so they must be allowed to live in that arena until they are willing to move on.

There is a mass belief that the outer world is more important than the inner world, and this is also undergoing change. There is a mass belief in scarcity, that there is not enough for everyone. This is one of the underlying beliefs of your civilization and is a source of competition and power struggles. No negative judgment is implied here; this is only an observation that some people learn in certain ways that make life hard for themselves. You can help bring in new thoughtforms, such as the thought that it is possible to grow through joy rather than through pain and struggle. I am calling your attention to mass beliefs you may subscribe to. Once you recognize them, you may choose whether you agree with them and want to live by them or not.

Are you willing to believe
in ideas of abundance,
of validating your inner world,
and of learning to grow through joy?

Starting with your own past, think of a time in which something happened you did not understand. Now, as you look back as an adult, as an older, more mature self, you can understand precisely why you drew that incident to you and what you learned from it. For instance, you can observe, as you look back with the larger picture in mind, that when you did not get what you thought you wanted, there was a reason for not having it. Perhaps not having it changed your life path. Maybe having it would have held you back in some way, or maybe the desire came from a smaller, less-evolved part of you. As you look back through your memories, reviewing past career paths and relationships (even those you are still in but letting go of), see how they served you. What you have now would not be possible without those experiences.

You cannot leave something until you love it. The more you hate something, the more you are bound to it; the more you love something, the freer you are. So as you love your past, you become free from it. When you can think of your childhood and your parents and know that they were perfect for the path you are on, you are then free of the effects of your past. As you change your negative memories into positive understanding, you can go even faster into your new future.

You can release the past by loving it.

Every time you think of a bad memory that makes you feel sorry for yourself, or bad about how you acted, or makes you think of yourself as a victim, stop! Reflect on what good you created from that experience. It may be that you learned so much from it you never again brought that kind of behavior back into your life. It may be that you changed your path because of that situation. It may have led to an important connection or to developing new qualities and personality traits. It may have been a job in which you served and helped many people.

Your parents may have developed your strength, or your inner will, by imposing their will on you or creating obstacles. People who want to develop muscles, for instance, may use weights to push against. Your parents may have acted as a "weight" for you to push against to develop your inner strength. Everything in your past happened for your good. If you can believe that the Universe is friendly, that it is always helping you to create your highest good, you can live a life of more peace and security.

Look at your present-time existence. If you wish to see the larger picture, sit and imagine going into the future. If you are facing a new challenge, one for which you have not yet acquired the necessary skills, imagine yourself going into the future and uniting with your future self, drawing to yourself the knowledge that future self holds. It may not come into your conscious awareness until the moment you need it, but your future self can send you energy and knowledge that can make what you are going through today seem easier.

If you are facing decisions or troubles, imagine yourself five years from now looking back at today, viewing the overall picture. Then link with that self of the future. From that perspective it would be much simpler to know what to do today. You could even imagine you are your future self, then share with your current self from that future perspective. It may seem as though you are making things up as you experience your future self telling you why you are going through what you are experiencing and affirming the rightness of everything that is happening. Your future self is real and separated from you only by time. It can talk to you and help you know what to do right now, how to get where you want to go even more quickly, and it often gets messages to you through your creative mind, your imagination.

When you imagine your future,
do not think you will be
the same then as you are now.

You will be more evolved, wiser, expanded; problems that exist now in your life will be solved. Problems create a focus of attention. They are labeled as problems because you do not yet have a solution, nor is that new part of you yet activated or matured that knows how to deal with the situation effectively. Often you create problems to originate new forms of behavior and evolve parts of yourself. You can do that without creating crisis, by paying attention to the whispers of your mind and by spending time imagining yourself in the future. You can draw to yourself new images of who you want to be, but also be willing to release the situations and things in your life that do not fit those images.

The emotional body has the most to gain from reframing everything into the positive, for every time you say a negative word to yourself or make yourself wrong, your emotional body changes its vibration and your energy drops. When the vibration becomes lower, your magnetism changes, and you attract to yourself people and events that amplify this drop in energy. Once you take responsibility and attune your awareness to higher thoughts, creating joyful images in your mind, you can raise the vibration of your emotional body. Then you will want to have people in your personal life who contribute to and share those high feelings. If you find, however, the people you know are constantly depressed or angry or in a negative emotional state, ask yourself what belief you have that says it is good for you to be around them.

Most of you have habits and patterns in your personal relationships that repeat themselves regardless of whom you are with. If you are willing to release those patterns, you will find many new ways of deepening the ties between you and others. If you focus on something that is wrong with another person, you can make it even larger. The things that were working in your relationship before will stop working. On the other hand, if you focus on bringing out the good in other people, seeing their beauty and sharing with them what you love about them, you will find the areas that were giving you problems begin to resolve themselves, even though you have not worked directly on finding solutions.

The more you focus on problems between you and others, or on what is wrong with other people, the more you will find your relationships going downhill. When people first get together, they are so focused on the good in each other it is said that they wear rose-colored glasses. This is a great gift to each other, for as each pays attention to the good in the other he or she helps the other create it.

> *Loving people is a commitment*
> *to hold a high vision of them,*
> *even as time and familiarity*
> *take their toll.*

Many of you, when you sense a difference between yourself and a loved one or friend, get into power struggles or competition to deal with it. If, instead, you accept another's worldview as simply different from yours, you will not need to do anything other than love him or her. You do not need to convince people you are right, for that only draws you into power struggles with them. Nor do you need to be convinced that they are right. Being positive does not mean being blind. It means being willing to recognize the good in others and to turn the focus away from what is different or wrong (to you).

The more you point out to others all the ways they are bad or wrong, the more insecure you make them, which actually creates and enlarges the problems you are focusing on. Or you can tell people in your life how good they are and help them recognize how much they are growing. Whenever others complain of a problem or something wrong, you can help them see how the situation is helping them, the positive changes it is giving them, and what it is teaching them.

You may be thinking of your job or lack of one as a problem, or wishing you could change your career or create a new one. Your higher self is always watching over you. It is always monitoring you to see if your attitudes — if who you are at the personality and the emotional and mental levels

— are developed enough to have what you want. If it sees you are not ready, it will offer you many growth opportunities to evolve those parts that need to be developed. You may need certain skills, to meet new people, or to change your environment.

> *Your higher self will guide you*
> *in the right direction so that you can*
> *make the changes you are asking for*
> *to have what you want.*

If you come from the larger perspective, you will understand that what is happening to you right now is preparing you for more. When you catch people complaining, simply say to them, "Stop." Learn to use your voice to halt people's energy when they start complaining. If you listen to people gripe, if you listen to their negativity, you put yourself in a position where you can be affected by their lower energy. You do not need to listen. By stopping people from telling you their stories, particularly if they are not good ones, you assist them in coming out of it. Pay attention and observe what people are talking about when you are with them. Do they go on and on about their sad stories? Are they acting like victims rather than taking responsibility for their part in what is happening? If so, you are connecting with them at the personality level, when you could be relating to them in a higher way.

Ask them what they want and where they are going. What higher purpose can they create? Refocus them on the positive, and you will be doing the same for yourself. Be willing to listen alertly to everyone who comes your way. Listen to conversations in public places. If you notice that they are not positive, tune them out. First, if you choose, mentally send people the thought that the level of development they are at now will evolve, and send love to them for who they are.

Notice the TV, newspapers, and books you read — do they use positive words? Do they bring up your energy or do they take it down and plant negative images in your mind? You are absolutely free to choose what you read and hear. No one makes you do anything. This week use that freedom and free will to put yourself in the highest, most supportive environment you can create. Observe and watch what level people are coming from. You will see that you have much to offer by helping others into a higher space. Know that you can carry light and bring it to all those people you contact.

Changing the Negative into the Positive
PLAYSHEET

1. Think of someone you have felt critical about lately. What did you feel especially critical of?

2. What do you criticize in yourself that is the same or the opposite of what you criticize in this person? For example, perhaps you criticize a friend for always being late. You may pride yourself about being on time, but find on closer examination that you are very critical of yourself concerning issues of time.

3. Think of a time you did the same thing for which you are criticizing the other person. For instance, say you are criticizing your friend for not returning money to you. Was there a time that you did not return money or something else you borrowed?

4. Think of a time you felt warm and loving. Get into that feeling. Now think of the person you are criticizing. How do you feel toward him or her as you view this person with a warm and loving feeling? As you see your friend through a loving and compassionate heart, do the same with yourself and forgive yourself for being critical.

5. Keep that warm and loving feeling. Think of what you have criticized yourself for. Do you feel more warm and loving toward your own behavior?

DAILY JOY PRACTICE

Setting your intention is a very important part of personal and spiritual transformation. Once you set your intention, the Universe will support you in bringing it about. Think of something coming up that you are worried will be a negative experience. Decide that you are going to have a more positive experience and make this your intention.

Ask the Universe and your soul, your innermost being, to assist you in recognizing how you could experience this situation or area in a more positive way and let go of any fear or negativity around it. Bring your thoughts about this situation up into the light of your innermost self. Imagine that your innermost self is assisting you in identifying what is positive and good about what may occur, helping you to recognize how the Universe is working for you and with you, even if on the surface it does not seem to be so. If you choose, ask to have more positive thoughts or to better understand how this situation is serving to make you stronger and wiser. Notice how the Universe supports you in fulfilling your intention to have more positive thoughts and feelings about this area or situation you are working on.

Make up your mind to be a positive person today. Picture yourself saying positive, uplifting things to the people you are with. Imagine changing any negative thoughts that appear in your mind to positive thoughts. Observe how your positive attitude changes your feelings about yourself and the world around you. As you affirm your intention to view the world in more positive ways, you will draw to you those people, events, and circumstances, including books, articles, and audio programs, that will lift you higher and raise your vibration.

AFFIRMATIONS

I face the world with optimism and hope for a better future.

I live an abundant life.

I focus upon what is good in my life,
and thus the good in my life increases.

Everything happens for my higher good.

I release negativity. I have a positive outlook.

I experience many positive, uplifting thoughts.

I am a good person.
I acknowledge all the goodness within me.

I release all sources of negativity in my life.

I create a positive, uplifting environment for myself.

I focus on what is positive and working well in my life.

I realize that all past circumstances, relationships,
and experiences made me a better person
and stronger in some way.

I love and appreciate people for who they are.
I have positive thoughts of others.

I have joyful pictures of the future.

I recognize all the good that other people
and the Universe are offering me.

The Universe is always working for me and with me.

I acknowledge what is good in people
and strengthen them by doing so.

I choose to focus on the good in the world,
and by doing so I help bring about a better world.

I speak to others about what is good
and positive in the world.

I speak about positive, uplifting things.
My words bring light to others.

CHAPTER FOUR

The Art of Self-Love

There are many ways you can love yourself, and everything that happens to you is an opportunity to have a loving experience. Seen in the right perspective, anything can provide you with an occasion to love yourself. When things seem to be going against you, they are only happening to show you blocks to your usable power. I am sure if I asked you to make a list of loving things to do for yourself, you would be able to think of many. Yet many times you focus on all the ways you are not carrying out those things, and a battle begins. This inner war can be draining, and making yourself wrong is not a right use of energy.

Loving yourself means
accepting yourself
as you are right now.

There are no exceptions to the contract, which is an agreement with yourself to appreciate, validate, accept, and support who you are at this moment. It means living in present time. Many of you look back to the past with regret, thinking of how you could have handled a situation in a higher way, imagining if only you had done this or that, things would have worked out better. Some of you look into the future to make who you are right now inadequate. The past can assist you if you remember the times in which you succeeded, creating positive memories. The future can be your friend if you see that in picturing it you are creating a vision of the next step. Do not make yourself wrong because you have not yet achieved your vision. It is important to love who you are now without reservation.

Loving yourself is beyond attachment and detachment. You exist in physical bodies, and each one of you has a focus that you call the "I." You have been given the "I" so you can separate from a greater whole and experience a particular part of beingness. Everything you have experienced up until now is what you were born to learn. Whether you label it good or bad, it is what composes your being, your uniqueness and purpose.

If you could see yourself from my perspective, you would view yourself as a crystal with many facets. Each of you is completely different, a unique combination of energy. Each of you is beautiful, special, and one of a kind, as is every crystal. You reflect light in a unique way, thus your aura varies from those around you. If you could appreciate your uniqueness, see that the path you have chosen is different from anyone else's, it would be easier to detach from the views of others and follow your own guidance.

One of the ways to love yourself more is to stop comparing yourself to others. Although you are part of a whole, you are also an individual self, with your own path. The group and family belief systems you have taken on as your own can be obstacles to your self-love. "Everybody says it is good to meditate," you may hear some people say, and so you feel bad if you do not do so. The challenge of loving yourself is to step aside from everything people tell you and ask, "Does this fit me? Does this bring me joy? Do I feel good when I do it?" Ultimately your own experience is what counts.

There is a temptation to make another person or some thing, such as a book, an authority and to put outside of yourself the ability to decide what is good for you. Being with teachers offers much benefit, but only so that eventually you can learn to bring in and follow your own guidance. I exist to open doors for you; I do not wish to take your power, but to give it to you. When you are with teachers or any person you have made an authority in your life, even if it is just a friend, question and listen carefully to what he or she is saying. You may accept his or her statements as truth, and yet it is important to question if what this person says is true just for him or her or if it is true for you also.

Loving yourself means stepping outside of guilt.

There is tremendous guilt in your society. Many connections between people come from the solar plexus, the power center, from which people try to persuade, convince, control, and manipulate each other. Loving yourself means stepping outside of these kinds of relationships. To do so you will need to let go of guilt. If you do not play the same ball game as those around you, you may find they feel threatened. They want you to think and act in certain ways to fit their pictures, so they try to gain power over you through guilt.

Often parents know no other way to be in control; they use guilt, anger, and the withdrawal of love to dominate their children. When you feel strong and in charge of your life, you can come from the heart. When you feel lacking in control, you may feel you must manipulate or engage in power struggles to get what you want. You may think you have to make excuses for your behavior or tell white lies to protect other people's feelings. When you act this way, you are not loving to yourself; instead you give your subconscious the message that who you are is not enough or acceptable to other people.

If you wish to be free, it is important not to manipulate other people either, but to give them their freedom. At first you may feel as if you have lost a measure of control if you turn over to other people the right to do as they please with their lives. You will create between you a completely new level of honesty and love that could not occur without your courage and willingness to release control.

You can learn to detach from the reactions of others and from your own emotions if they take you out of a calm, clear center. Loving yourself means asserting yourself with compassion. When you are willing to show others who you are, you open the door for them to expose their real selves also.

Judgment stands as an obstacle to self-love. Every time you judge, you separate. When you form opinions about another person, looking at him or her and saying, for instance, "This person is lazy, or a failure, or has terrible clothes," you send a message to your subconscious that the world is a place where you had better act in certain ways if you want to be accepted. By rejecting other people through your judgments, you inform your own subconscious that you are only going to accept yourself under certain conditions. This leads to an inner dialogue of self-criticism. It can also attract many negative images from the outer world, for once you send out these pictures, you create a pathway for them to come back.

Look at the messages you put out to other people. Do you accept them lovingly, without criticizing or putting them down? Do you smile at them? Are you friendly? Do you allow them to feel good about themselves, or do you walk away without acknowledging them? If you accept them, even just telepathically (that is, in your own mind), you assist them in finding their higher selves. You will find other people accepting you more lovingly also.

Your beliefs about reality
create your experience of it.

This dynamic can happen in subtle ways. If you think people do not accept you as you are, and that you must try hard to please them, then you will draw those kinds of people into your life. You may find that you end up seeing friends at the times they are tired and do not have anything to give. Whatever you believe to be true about friends or any person in your life, you will create that experience of them. If you say and believe, "This man or woman is warm and friendly toward me," you will create that in the relationship.

To move into a higher sense of self-love, start identifying what you consider to be facts about the way the world works. If you think that the world is cold and uncaring, or that you must try hard for everything you achieve, then that conviction stands between you and self-love. A belief is what you consider to be a truth about reality. You may say, "It is a fact that if I smile at people, they smile back," but this can be a reality for you and not for other people. Indeed, because of this belief, you may choose subconsciously to smile only at people who will smile back. If you believe that people never smile back at you, then you will automatically pick people to smile at who never return it.

If you want to experience a world that is caring and supports your images of self-love, look at what you are saying about the world to yourself. You can change your encounters with people and the world by altering what you expect. It has been said, "The world may not be just, but it is exact." This means that what you get is precisely what you expect and believe you will get. If you are in a profession you "know" is hard to make money in, and you say, "Not many people make money in my field," you will create that as a fact for yourself. You are holding a certain view of reality, and that will be your experience, not only of your career, but also of others you meet in that field. All you need do is alter what you expect to happen, and you will experience a different world.

Another quality of self-love is forgiveness. Some of you hang on to old issues, feeling anger over and over. It is irritation at yourself, perhaps, or at another who let you down. The higher self knows only forgiveness. If there is anything you are hanging on to — anger, hurt, or a negative feeling about another — then you are keeping it in your aura. The person you are mad at is affected, but not as much as you will be. Any energy or feelings you carry toward another person sits in your aura and acts as a magnet for more of the same. There is most definitely a reason for forgiveness, for it cleanses and heals you and changes for the better the circumstances you draw to yourself.

Self-love also involves humility, which is self-expression from the heart and not from the ego. Humility says, "I am open. I am willing to listen. I may not have all the answers." Humility is one of the qualities that will allow you to receive more, for humility implies openness. It does not imply a lack of self-confidence, but a great amount of faith and trust in yourself.

> *Only those who feel good*
> *about who they are*
> *can express humility.*

Those who act the most arrogant or coldly confident are those who lack the very characteristics they are trying to project. People who love themselves come across as very loving, generous, and kind; they express their self-confidence through humility, forgiveness, and inclusiveness. If you know people who seem to be very wise and yet put others down, reject friends, and make people feel bad about themselves — no matter how high their words or what they teach — you can rest assured they do not love themselves.

Loving yourself involves faith and trust and belief in who you are, and a willingness to act upon your trust in yourself. It is not enough to feel that faith and trust; you need to experience it in your outer world. You are a physical being, and joy comes from seeing around you those things that express your inner beauty — a garden, flowers, trees, your house, the ocean. All of these are the rewards of acting upon and trusting yourself, of following your path and vision with action. The ultimate challenge of self-love is to act upon it, to speak up to people and to create in the world your heaven on earth.

It is not enough just to give and radiate love; loving yourself comes from receiving love also. If you are giving love to people but they cannot receive it, then it has no place to go.

You do everyone a great service by being willing to receive their love.

*One of the greatest gifts
you can give others is opening
to their love for you.*

In any male-female relationship, or between two men or two women, the relationship will succeed to the degree to which each can receive the other's love. Even if you are giving 100 percent, if the other person is receiving only 50 percent, then what you give to the other is reduced by half. If what the other gives back is only 50 percent, and if you can only receive 50 percent of that, then what you get back is 25 percent, and so on. The result is that you experience less and less love from each other. To experience greater love in your life, be willing to receive gifts from others, offerings of love, friendship, and support.

If you want to bring your higher self into your life on a daily basis and increase your self-love, take one characteristic of the soul and, whenever you have a moment, think about it. Some of these are peace, appreciation, humility, harmony, joy, gratefulness, abundance, freedom, serenity, strength, integrity, respect, dignity, compassion, forgiveness, will, light, creativity, grace, wisdom, and love. By reflecting or meditating on these qualities, you will begin to demonstrate them in your life. Whatever you think of, you are. If every day you pick one of the qualities of your higher self to ponder on and identify with, you will create it as an experience of yourself.

Self-love involves respecting yourself and living in higher purpose. When you value yourself, your time, love, and vision, so will others. Before you see your friends, ask yourself, what is the highest purpose you can create together? Have you ever stayed at someone's house while really wanting to leave, but you hesitated, not wanting to hurt his or her feelings? If so, you were valuing that person more than yourself. You were giving him or her the telepathic message that he or she does not have to respect you or your time, and it should be no surprise if this person took you for granted after a while.

Whenever you value and respect yourself, speaking with truth about who you are and taking appropriate actions, you not only evolve yourself, but you assist others by your example. The inability to say no to people reflects a worldview that says other people's feelings are more important than yours, that their rights are more significant, and that you should consider their feelings first. When you do this you create energy blockages within yourself, backing up resentment, anger, and hurt, which then sit in your aura and attract more of the same.

Self-love comes from the heart and can be expressed as gentleness and unconditional love. Some people think self-love means acting powerful and using their power and personal will in an aggressive way that denies the rights of others. You have seen people who get their way and who do not care about their effect on others. You call them ruthless or inconsiderate. Often, in a similar way, you can be aggressive with yourself, one part of yourself dominating and controlling the other parts.

Sometimes, the personal will acts as if it were an enemy, trying to force, direct, or make you do certain things. It can feel like a parent standing over you. To make matters worse, you may think that the things it is trying to force you to do are for your highest good. For instance, you may constantly berate yourself for not being more organized, or for putting off something you feel you should start or finish. You may make huge lists of things to do and then feel bad if you do not get them done. This is making the personality right and your other self wrong, the self that is resisting the direction of your personal will. In this case, you are using your personal will against yourself. Your higher self may have created the resistance to keep you from doing certain things and is directing you to other paths and possibilities that hold more joy.

If you use your personal will in conjunction with the heart to help you in following a path you love, your personal will can assist you to increase your self-love. The personal will can be a director of focus. When you link it with what you love, there is no end to what is possible or to the boundaries you can transcend. Have you noticed that when you love to do something — say, your favorite hobby — you can work for hours on end and can easily say no to distractions? The personal will is a force like a river. You can either flow with it or swim against it. You can use it either to draw you toward your higher path or to constantly punish yourself for apparent transgressions. Which system motivates you? Is your personal will helping you increase your self-love by focusing you on your path and higher purpose and creating the intent and motivation for action?

Last but not least, do not take yourself so seriously.

Laugh and play. It is not the end of the world if something does not go right. The quality of humor is perhaps one of the greatest doorways to self-love. The ability to laugh, to smile at others, and to put your problems into perspective is an evolved skill. Those who come from a high level of self-love are often humorous, have a great wit, and love to bring out the childlike playfulness in others. They are willing to be spontaneous, often find reasons to smile, and are able to make others feel at ease and to be happy themselves.

As you observe the people in your life, ask yourself (and do it without judgment), do these people love themselves? If you are experiencing difficulties with them, look at the problem area and ask, do they love themselves in this area? Send them compassion to use in whatever way creates their highest good, and enjoy the love you have just sent out as it comes back to you to use for your highest good.

The Art of Self-Love

PLAYSHEET

1. How would you know if you were acting or thinking in a way that is loving to yourself?

2. How would today or tomorrow look if everything you did was an act of self-love?

3. What would your actions look like if you were loving to yourself in the following areas: your physical body, your intimate relationship, your job or career?

4. What would you do today or tomorrow to be more loving to yourself in your relationships, in your job, and with your physical body? Think of three specific actions you would take for each of these three areas.

DAILY JOY PRACTICE

Sense your energy for a moment, allowing yourself to come into the center of your being. Open to experience a deeper part of your being, your innermost self, whose nature is pure, unconditional love.

This self, your soul, loves you, understands you, and is always working for your higher good. Ask your soul to increase the love you are capable of receiving. Allow the love that is within the core of your being to become more visible and shine forth, increasing your ability to love yourself.

As you think of the day ahead, picture feeling more of the love that is within you and finding new ways to express it. Something within you is growing stronger, wiser, and more loving as you open to the unlimited love within you. As you go about your day, imagine that your innermost self is bringing you all the opportunities you need to love, nurture, and honor yourself, and then do so.

Practice loving yourself today with your thoughts and your words. Make yourself right rather than wrong. Forgive yourself, knowing that you are always doing the best you know how. Make yourself the authority of what is good for you. Feel the joy that comes from honoring who you are. At night, reflect on how the day felt and what changed as you opened to a new level of self-love.

AFFIRMATIONS

I do those things that are loving to myself.

I release anything that is not for my higher good.

I appreciate, value, and accept myself for who I am.

I have positive memories.
I remember times when I succeeded.

I let go of the past and focus on creating a loving,
wonderful future.

I appreciate, accept, support, and validate who I am
with my thoughts, feelings, and words.

I love myself without reservation.

I am the authority of what is good for me.

I assert myself with confidence and compassion.

I believe in myself.

I come from my heart.

I laugh and play. I have a smile in my heart.

I support other people in feeling good about themselves.

I forgive myself, knowing I am always doing
the best I know how.

I forgive other people, knowing they are always doing the best they know how.

People love and accept me for who I am.

I experience smiles and friendly faces everywhere I go.

I receive love easily, and others give it to me generously.

CHAPTER FIVE

Self-Respect, Self-Esteem, and Self-Worth

W hat is required to feel good about yourself is not the same from person to person. What you require for self-esteem is not necessarily what another person requires. It is important to discover what makes you feel worthy, confident, and happy about who you are.

Self-respect at the highest levels comes from honoring your soul. This means speaking and acting from a level of integrity and honesty that reflects your higher self. It means standing by what you believe in (you do not, however, have to convince others to believe in it), and acting in a way that reflects your values. Many of you criticize others for not living up to a value system you consider right, but on closer examination you may not be living up to it yourself. You have seen the person who is always telling people how they should act, but he or she does anything he or she pleases. Self-respect means acting on your values and what you say you believe in.

Professing one set of values but acting from another leads to a lot of internal conflict. For instance, you may believe in

monogamy deep inside, and yet the person you are with wants
an open relationship. You decide to go along because you want
to hold on to this partner. You believe in one set of values, but
you are living by another, and there will be a lot of conflict and
potential pain around this issue.

How can you know if the values you "think" you want to
live by are yours? You often cannot know until you try. You
might think that a good person gets up early in the morning,
yet you always sleep late. Many of you have values you think
you should live by but do not. The best thing to do is to try
out these values — get up early in the morning for a while.
Often, what you think are your values turn out to be "shoulds"
given to you by others, and when you actually live them, you
find they do not work for you. Ask yourself what you value.
What do you think *good* people do? Are you following these
values? It is difficult to feel good about yourself if you are
living in a way that goes against your underlying values. It is
important to examine your values and either live by them or
change them.

Self-respect means coming from your power, not your weakness.

When you complain that someone or something is making
you sad or angry, ask yourself, "Why am I choosing to experience that feeling or to react in that way?" Blaming others will
always take away your power. If you can discover why you are
choosing to feel hurt by other people's actions, you will learn
much about yourself. Some of you are afraid that if you stand
up for yourself, you will lose someone's love. Some people
are quite good at convincing you that you are in the wrong
when you do stand up for your beliefs. Thank them silently

for providing you with the opportunity to become strong, for often strength is developed in the face of opposition. Self-respect means standing by your deepest truth and knowing your innermost feelings. It means making yourself and not another the authority of your feelings.

Some of you live or associate with people who belittle you and make you feel bad. You can end up focusing so much on their feelings that you lose track of your own. A woman was married to a man who constantly criticized many of her actions. She became so focused on his feelings that she never asked herself during all the years they were together how she felt about the way he treated her. She was always trying hard to please him, trying to anticipate his moods and whims in order to avoid his criticism. Yet everything she tried ended with him being angry or irritated at her. She began to feel she had failed or was in some way a bad person. She spent so many hours analyzing his feelings that she lost touch with her own. Many of you try to please people, and as you try to please them, you focus more on how they feel than how you feel.

Self-worth means paying attention to how *you* feel. You do not need reasons why you choose to do something. You do not need to prove anything to another person about your worth. Validate your feelings; do not analyze and question them. Do not go over and over them, asking, "Do I really have a reason to feel hurt?" Let your feelings be real for you and honor them. Many of you make other people the authority of what is good for you. When they say you are bad, you believe them. When they say things are your fault, you believe them. I am not suggesting that you ignore what other people say, either, but instead honor what *you* feel. It is one thing to be open to constructive criticism and another to constantly try to do what others want you to do when you do not want it for yourself.

Creating self-esteem and self-worth involves honoring your own feelings and path and direction. It means honoring yourself with your words, actions, and behavior.

Self-esteem means believing in yourself, knowing that you did the best you knew how, even though two days later you might see a better way. It involves making yourself right rather than wrong and allowing yourself to feel good about who you are. Some of you try very hard all the time, pushing yourselves, rushing around and feeling that whatever you do, it is not enough. Trying and working hard to get things done is not necessarily the road to joy. Respect yourself by following your inner flow. Rest, play, think, and take time to be silent. Doing those things that nurture yourself are ways to increase your self-esteem.

How you treat yourself is how others will treat you.

Do not wait for other people to respect you or treat you in a more positive way. They will not until you treat yourself with respect. You do not have to be around people who do not honor you, respect you, or treat you well. If you do find yourself around those kinds of people, act with dignity and remember that they are not respecting you because they do not respect themselves. You can telepathically send out a message about how you want to be treated. Others only take advantage of you and take you for granted if you let them.

You do not need to get angry or demand your rights, for that only creates a power struggle between you and others. Keep your heart open. They most likely cannot recognize their own greater selves, and so it is not possible for them to honor yours. You do not want to base your self-esteem upon how others treat you or view you. No matter how good you feel about yourself, there will always be those who do not treat you in a respectful way, for they have not learned how to treat themselves in a loving way. The relationships you have with others can only be as good as the relationships they have with themselves. If they do not know how to love themselves, that limits how much they can love you. No matter how hard you try, how many nice things you do, they cannot give you the love you seek. Forgiveness is the key to feeling good about how others treat you. Then, release any anger you may feel; simply let it go and focus on other things.

Some of you feel your parents are responsible for your lack of self-esteem. You cannot blame your parents, as it was your reaction to them that created any lack of confidence. Two children may come from equally abusive or negative parents, and one will grow up feeling good about himself or herself, and the other will not. You make the decision to feel bad. Rather than feeling sorry for yourself about your childhood or feeling like a victim of your upbringing, realize your soul chose to put you in that situation to learn something that would assist your growth. One of the lessons you may have come to learn in this lifetime is how to love and honor yourself, so you create situations that challenge yourself to do so. As soon as you decide to love and honor yourself, the pattern will end.

Some people might say, "I have a pattern of people abusing me because of my abusive father." In this case, those people came to earth to learn something about love, and if they do not learn it from their father, they will put themselves around people with similar patterns to teach them what they need to learn. For instance, they may have experienced their father as abusive, and then found that they were attracted to similar

types of people until one day they decided they would no
longer allow others to treat them that way.

*Every situation in your life
is a learning experience
created by your soul
to teach you how to gain
more love and power.*

Children respond in different ways to the same upbringing,
as you can see when you observe how different brothers and
sisters may be, even though they have the same parents. Some
children respond to the negative energy around them by
becoming loving and gentle. Some are so sensitive that they
cannot stand feeling negative energy and will shut down, not
wanting to feel anything. Some respond by feeling that they
must be hard and so they project an image of invulnerability.
Self-esteem comes from being willing to acknowledge who you
are and love yourself just as you are right now. It is difficult to
change until you accept who you are. When you honor yourself and your feelings, others' judgments and opinions cannot
affect you.

You are a worthy individual, no matter what your past, no
matter what your thoughts, no matter who believes in you.
You are life itself, growing, expanding, and reaching upward.
All people are valuable, beautiful, and unique. Every experience you have is meant to teach you more about creating love
in your life.

There is a fine line between respecting yourself and being
selfish. Some of you feel you have every right to get angry with
others because they hurt you. Honor your feelings, but do so

in such a way that you also honor the feelings of others. To accomplish this you will want to come from a high level of speaking and thinking. Speaking of your anger with others, yelling and screaming, only creates a power struggle with others and closes everyone's heart. When someone does something you do not like, open your heart before you speak. If you choose to make a statement, state what you feel about the situation, rather than blame someone for something they did to you. You can say, "I feel hurt," rather than, "*You* hurt me." A powerful way to state this is, "I am *choosing* to feel hurt," for every feeling you have is one you have chosen.

> *Self-worth is knowing*
> *that you are choosing your feelings*
> *at every moment.*

When you communicate to other people in a way that honors their deeper being, you always feel better about yourself. You may notice that when you get something off your chest by expressing anger or hurt, you often feel worse afterward. At the very least, there is a sense of incompletion. You cannot leave a situation until you have done so with love. Those situations you leave in anger will be there for you to resolve in the future. It may not be with the same person, but you will create a similar situation with another person that allows you to resolve it with peace and love.

It is important to respect others. If you do not feel respected by others, you may have put yourself in that situation to learn how to have compassion and gentleness in *your* treatment of other people. Being sensitive to other people's feelings is different from trying to please them. Be willing to see their needs and desires. Do you speak curtly to others without paying attention to their feelings? Do you speak with annoyance or irritation? Watch the energy you put out to other people, for whatever you put out you will get back. Become more aware of your effect on other people, for the more you respect them, the more you will receive respect. Honor their worth, their time, and their values, and you will find them honoring yours.

Some people honor other people all the time and feel they do not get back what they give. In this case, often they do not feel they deserve to be treated well, and they allow people to take them for granted. It is easy to respect yourself when others respect you. The challenge is to respect yourself when those around you do not. First, forgive them, and then let go of any need for them to validate you. When you need other people to validate, appreciate, or understand you to feel good about yourself, you give away your power.

It feels good when other people believe in you, trust you, and support you. Yet, if you want to be powerful, it is important not to *need* other people to do so as a condition of believing in yourself. The need for constant validation makes other people the authority and not your own true self. Your truth may not be the same as other people's truth. The only wrong is when you do not honor your truth and accept what is true for another even though it is not true for you. Some people believe in reincarnation, and some people do not. It may be that a belief in reincarnation makes life more joyful and easier to live. It may be that a belief that there are no other lifetimes makes this one more important and real. Whatever belief you hold, it is important that you honor it and be open to new ways of seeing things if they create more joy in your life. Do not automatically accept something unless it has the ring of truth for you. Honor your truth, believe in and stand up for yourself, but have compassion for other people.

Remember that you count, you are important, and that you have a unique and special contribution to make to the world. Know that you are a special being. Your dreams, fantasies, and goals are as important as those of anyone else.

Self-Respect, Self-Esteem, and Self-Worth
PLAYSHEET

1. Think of a pattern you seem to experience with people over and over.

2. Get quiet, relax, and go within. Ask your deeper, wiser self to show you what you are learning from this. How is it teaching you to respect and love yourself more?

3. What soul qualities are you developing from this situation? For instance, you may be developing the quality of compassion, honesty, speaking your deepest truth, peace, self-love, humility, harmlessness, taking responsibility for your actions, and so on.

4. Would you be willing to learn these same lessons and to develop these qualities through growing with joy instead of repeating this pattern over and over? If so, make this your intention, affirm that you are ready to release this pattern as a way to grow, and open to new, more joyful ways to evolve.

DAILY JOY PRACTICE

Make a commitment to respect and honor yourself and your truth. Decide to view every situation that comes your way today as an opportunity to do so. Increase your ability to honor yourself with your actions and words by coming into alignment with your soul, your innermost self.

Let your soul flood your entire personality with feelings of self-esteem, self-worth, and self-respect. Feel your soul increasing your ability to believe in yourself and treat yourself with respect.

Think of the day ahead. Picture that, before you deal with people or situations, you will take a moment to center yourself and align with the highest part of your being. As you do this, imagine your soul strengthening your ability to know your true, innermost self and to speak and act in ways that are in alignment with it.

Picture yourself interacting with people in ways that affirm your worth, respect your feelings, and honor who you are deep within. Think of how you will feel at the end of the day when you act in this way. Notice that as you respect yourself, others respect you also. Today decide that you are worthy and give yourself permission to be true to who you are with every word you say and every interaction you have.

AFFIRMATIONS

I align with my innermost self often throughout the day.

I treat myself with respect.

I do things that nurture me.

I believe in myself.

I pay attention to and honor my feelings.

I take responsibility for how I feel.

I follow my inner flow throughout the day.

My heart is open.

I feel good about myself.

I honor my values with my words and thoughts.

I am worthy.

I value myself.

I respect and honor other people.

I choose to be around people who honor and respect me.

I act in ways that promote feelings of self-worth
and self-esteem.

I make wise use of my time and energy.

I trust my inner wisdom.

I believe in my unlimited capacity to create whatever I want.

I honor my deepest truth with my words,
actions, and behavior.

CHAPTER SIX

Refining the Ego: Recognizing Who You Are

I t is important to recognize who you are, without being too egotistical or too humble. It is the twofold problem of being all you can be. Many of you have not developed a picture of power that you would want to emulate. Many of your images and role models of powerful people come from those who have abused and misused their influence. Therefore, many of you have held back from using your power because the images you hold of it are negative.

> *It is important to develop positive pictures about the nature of power.*

Many of you are very evolved, loving, and wise and are looking for ways to express these qualities in the outer world. Learn to tell the difference between people who are truly influential and full of light and those who only wear the cloak of power. This skill will assist you on your path of joy, for it will also help you to recognize your own nobility, goodness, and wisdom. Think now of a person you consider powerful, male or female. What is it about that person that you admire?

You all know people who have a great deal of authority, and yet when you are with them, you feel depreciated, ignored, or put down. I speak of those people who seem to be in a position of power and control and who have many people around them. I will say that true power is the ability to motivate, love, encourage, and assist people in recognizing who they are.

Think now of people you know who have changed your life. In knowing them, you felt inspired and expanded. Think of how they used their influence. It is important to recognize people who are full of light, for they come in many forms and packages. It is time to be aware of those people who are leading you to a path of greater light and joy. If you can clearly identify those people who have your greatest good in mind, and surround yourself with them, you will grow more rapidly and have much more to offer others.

Evolved people are usually very gentle souls. Some evolved souls do not yet recognize who they are and may be too humble. They are most often generous, helpful, and friendly. It may seem as if they cannot do enough for you.

At a certain level of development where the personality does not yet recognize the level of the soul, people may be too humble, still wearing the cloak of self-doubt, of wondering who they are. You who are so kind and loving, yet too humble and full of doubts, are also full of light; you have so much to offer the world. It is important for you to take off your veil, for it hinders you in serving on a larger scale. When you pay attention to your doubts and fears, to that little voice saying, "You are not good enough," you are simply giving heed to your lower self. You have the ability to change your focus.

*Pay attention to your higher nature,
and your lower one will simply
wither from lack of attention.*

You do not need to pay attention to those voices within you that create pain or make you feel less competent, smart, or able. You can simply act as if that part of you were a small child; hold it, reassure it, and move on. Do not let those voices attract too much of your attention, and do not think that you are them, either. Learn not to pay attention to the little voices within that would have you think you are not great.

The basic nobility of your soul is seeking expression in your actions. What qualities or personality traits would you like to have? Which character traits do you already have about which you feel good? Realize that the qualities you would like to embody, you already have. You are simply looking for an increased expression of them in your life.

There is a fine line between being egotistical and being confident. Walking that line brings the expression of power into balance. Do you brag about yourself? Do you go around telling people when you do something great? Or do you listen to people with an open ear, putting your own accomplishments aside? The tendency to overstate or exaggerate accomplishments can create problems. Do you find yourself rehearsing what you are going to say to someone about something wonderful you accomplished? There is a difference between coming from confidence and coming from egotism.

If you feel you have done or are doing something great or unusual, you are telling your subconscious that this is not a normal achievement. If you want to bring more great accomplishments into your life, then take them in stride when they happen. (Congratulate yourself as if this were something you did every day.) For instance, some of you go on diets. When you succeed for one or two days, you tell yourself how wonderfully you did. Thus you tell your subconscious that this is an extraordinary occurrence and not a normal one.

If you want to change your nutritional habits, and you eat healthy food for a day or two, treat this as if it were something you do every day, rather than a great and unusual deed. Take your accomplishment in stride. You will then create a vision of healthful eating as your normal mode of being. Later, however, when this way of life has become established, do let yourself feel good about the change you have made.

There are times when you need to congratulate yourself far more than you do. This is the other side of the coin, not too much egotism, but the lack of it. Some of you achieve your goals and never stop to acknowledge or congratulate yourselves; you simply focus on the next thing you must do. You lack awareness of your achievements and do not acknowledge the things you do that work well in your life.

It is important to become aware when you focus on what you are not. You may say, "I need to do this or that. Why am I always so unorganized, so unfocused?" Be aware that as you focus on your lack of certain qualities, you are rejecting and weakening the qualities that you want to develop.

Whatever you pay attention to is what you create.

If you spend time feeling bad about something you did, feeling that you were not powerful, or that you did not say the right thing, or if you focus on the things you are not, you increase their power over you. Instead, recognize the qualities you have. Take the things you want to become, and remember those times when you demonstrated those qualities. The more you see within yourself what you want to become, the more you will become it.

If you say to yourself, "I have no willpower; I never get things done," then you are simply sending that energy out into the future. If, on the other hand, you say to yourself, "I love the way I act around people; I have so much willpower; I am so focused," you will experience a new energy coming up from within. You will find yourself expressing those qualities. Every time you have a negative image of yourself — saying things such as, "I never get things done; I do not have enough time" — you send out an image to the world, broadcast that quality, and create that circumstance in your life. If you say positive things about yourself, you will become them also.

Very enlightened and evolved souls know how to show their greatness and power and not create defensiveness, but devotion. If you want people to respect and look up to you, know that it will not happen because you walk around telling everyone how great you are. You have seen people who do that; they invite attack. You have also seen people who are truly evolved, who smile, who recognize greatness in other people, whose focus is assisting and helping. That is true power. It comes from the inner image you hold of yourself. You do not need to tell people if you are peaceful or focused — they know it. Communication is telepathic.

The images you send out
about yourself into the world
determine how other people see you.

If you walk around telling people something about your-self you do not feel is true, people will sense it. On the other hand, if you know that you have a particular quality or person-ality trait, everywhere you go people will recognize it in you and support you for it, even if you do not tell them about it.

A refined ego has the ability to get along with other people, to assist them in seeing their nobility and power. Competition often comes from those who do not see who they are, who do not trust in their inner greatness. It comes from a lack of confi-dence. When you are truly secure, when you know and experi-ence the abundance available, there is no need to compete. You will instead help others create abundance in their lives, be it money, love, or success. You will want to assist others in seeing who they are because you have all you need and recog-nize who you are.

When you are with your friends, are you concerned about what they think of you? If you want them to respect and look up to you, then spend time listening to them. Help them focus on their highest good; assist them in seeing their beauty and inner light. People who have true power are not concerned with the impression they make. They are more interested in the person they are with than themselves. They find their sense of inner peace increasing.

Many of you have been afraid
to assert your power
because of your mistaken and
negative images of power.

There is a need for more role models and leaders who are examples of positive authority. Many of your great spiritual leaders have come to show new images of power, refined spiritual power. An influential person is someone who has linked their personal will with a higher Will and who can direct his or her personal will to higher good. That is true power. Someone who is concerned with assisting and healing others is demonstrating spiritual power. Even if people speak profound words and talk about wise things, if you do not feel increased and expanded when you are with them, as if you have gained access to a deeper level of your being, then you have not experienced true power.

If you want the people around you to experience your power and recognize who you are, listen to them with your heart and do not worry about the impression you are making on them. Care about them and attend to them. Pay attention with your heart, and focus on how you may raise their consciousness and energy. You can see true power in the eyes. There is such love in the eyes of those who are truly powerful, and they look at you directly. They do not avoid your eyes, but look straight into them. You feel they really care about you. They pay attention to what you are saying. Do you give that kind of alert awareness to people? Do you pay attention? Do you look in their eyes when you speak? Do you listen to what they say or are you busy constructing your reply or thinking of a defense? Does your mind frequently wander to other things while others are talking? Pay attention with your heart; listen to the unspoken words, for these are ways to develop your power.

Look at those people who are nice and gentle, who cannot do enough for you or give you enough love. Increase those people in your life; draw them to you. You have heard the expression "The meek shall inherit the earth." It means that true power is expressed through humility. Truly powerful people have great humility. They do not try to impress; they do not try to be influential. They simply are. People are magnetically drawn to them. They are most often very silent and focused, aware of their core selves. They know that everything in the outer Universe is simply symbolic of their inner worlds. They are in charge of their destinies, and they often have many people seeking them out for advice. People feel recharged and regenerated by their contact. They do not try to convince anyone of anything; they only invite and offer. They never persuade, nor do they use manipulation or aggressiveness to get their way. They listen. If there is anything they can offer to assist you, they offer it; if not, they are silent.

Look around at the role models you have chosen, and redefine power in your life. See it as that gentle flowing river of energy that your soul is directing. Become aware of who you are. Broadcast to the Universe positive, loving images about yourself and watch people respond. Be willing to use your higher qualities and recognize your abilities.

Refining the Ego: Recognizing Who You Are
PLAYSHEET

1. Think of two people you know who have really made a difference in your life, who have encouraged, loved, and motivated you, or left you feeling inspired and expanded.

2. Think of two people for whom you did the same. See yourself as possessing the qualities that inspire, motivate, encourage, and expand others.

3. What qualities or character traits do you have that you would like to be able to express more of, such as compassion, wisdom, peace, joy, balance, security? State as many as you can think of as if those qualities were growing and expanding. For example, "My compassion is expanding every day."

4. Select one person or situation in which to practice expressing one of those qualities this week.

Daily Joy Practice

Today, if you choose, practice relating to other people and to yourself in ways that recognize who you are beyond the ego, that honor your innermost being and the innermost being of others.

To create a shift for yourself in your ability to relate to others beyond the ego, connect with the innermost part of your being. Open to receive the love, compassion, wisdom, understanding, gentleness, and humility that lie within you and are the essence of who you are.

Think of someone you will be with today. Imagine looking directly into this person's eyes as you speak. You listen to whatever this person says with your full attention. You release any thoughts of yourself and instead focus on the other person. Your heart is open. You acknowledge his or her nobility with your thoughts, words, and actions.

You can be a source of support, encouragement, and inspiration to this person and to everyone you will be with today. Today you are choosing to relate to others from this higher level of unity, caring, and love, experiencing more of who you are deep within as you do.

Sense how kind, loving, and full of light you are as you let go of the ego and open to express who you are deep within. Know that as you do this you are opening the way for others to recognize how kind, loving, and full of light they are as well. Sense a new level of connection between you and others as you honor who you are and as you respect and honor the other person. Imagine the joy and peace you will feel at the end of the day, knowing that you offered kindness and loving energy to everyone around you.

AFFIRMATIONS

I recognize the light within me and
humbly acknowledge my nobility.

I express power with love and wisdom.

I have much to offer the world.

I am competent, smart, and able.

I am kind, loving, and full of light.

I recognize the many good qualities I have.

I focus on what I am doing well.

I say positive things to myself.

I surround myself with people who have
my greatest good in mind.

I recognize the many good qualities others have within them.

I listen to people with an open heart and ear.

I am fully present with others when I am with them.

I release any thoughts of what I lack and
focus instead on all that I have.

I acknowledge the beauty and light in others.

I assist others in recognizing and expressing
their beauty and inner light.

I motivate, encourage, and support people
in recognizing who they are.

I inspire people.

CHAPTER SEVEN

Subpersonalities:
Uniting the Separated Selves

You have various roles and identities, which I will call your "subpersonalities." These roles exist within all of you. For instance, one part of you might be impulsive and do things without thinking, and another part might be careful and cautious. One part may not like other people to be angry with you, and another may want people to need you. A part of you may be afraid, creating fears of the future, or an obsessive part might remember painful situations and call them to your attention frequently. You are bringing each one of these parts, in your journey through this lifetime, to a higher level of knowing and understanding.

Learning not to identify with your subpersonalities as being the real you frees you and assists you in bringing them to the light. The journey into the higher self is the integration of all the selves, or subpersonalities, with the soul. The voice that tells you that you cannot do something, when your inner guidance is encouraging you to do it, is usually not the voice of the higher self. It is simply a part of you that you need to recognize and love, to show it your higher vision.

With your higher vision, you can heal and integrate the selves that exist within you. Perhaps you created them during times of crisis, or they are based on images of reality and programs of instruction passed on to you from parents or friends. For instance, say you keep attracting what you feel are the wrong relationships into your life. A subpersonality may be bringing you relationships based on an old image. Maybe your parents in some way rejected you, so a subpersonality formed an image of rejection as an element of being loved. This self may be very good at bringing you friends — so you can acknowledge that it is trying to do something positive for you, even though your friends at some point reject you.

Do not judge yourself if you are repeating certain patterns over and over, for clearing those patterns is one of the ways you evolve. It is time now to become aware of this self, talk to it, and give it a new image of what kind of love you want. For instance, you may have a self that believes in scarcity — that there is not enough love or money, and so on. It would be good to talk to this part of you, showing it images of abundance.

Think for a moment, if you had six months to live, what would be the most important thing you would want to finish and leave behind? What would you change about your life right now? What limits do you have now that you would do away with? If you were to leave behind one gift to the planet, what would it be?

*You have a part of you
that looks over and
observes your other
parts — that is your higher self.*

The greatest movement to the higher self comes both in acknowledging the higher self and in evolving all the other parts. Your subpersonalities are simply parts of you that you have not yet aligned with your innermost, higher self. You can very easily change the images these parts are holding by first paying attention to the voices within you. When you hear a certain thought pattern, such as a doubtful voice, begin to see it as a part of you that is asking for help from your soul, as a part that needs to be shown new images and belief systems. You can respond to any of the voices that you know are not your higher self by listening to them and showing them your higher vision. They simply are not aware that you have changed the model by which you are creating reality.

What is this higher purpose, this higher vision? All of you came into incarnation not only to achieve certain levels of evolution but also to help with the planet, to contribute to the well-being of all life. When things happen effortlessly and doors open, it is because not only are you on your own higher path but you are weaving it into the higher vision of life on earth. You are here to evolve certain qualities within yourself and to manifest your higher purpose. You can know what those qualities are by looking at what challenges continually present themselves to you. They may seem like separate situations, and yet there is a pattern to what you are learning in your life and the lessons you are attracting.

Everyone is born with a higher purpose and vision. Your journey through this lifetime is to find and fulfill that vision. The challenge to your higher self is to constantly enlarge your vision of who you are and to put that evolved self in more and more expansive arenas. Some of you may specialize in one specific thing, focusing on it in great detail. For others your path may be to reach out into new areas to acquire knowledge.

Interweaving all the parts of your being into a greater whole, becoming your higher self, is one of the goals of your soul in its evolutionary cycle.

The higher self is the part of you that is beyond the world of polarities. Your subpersonalities exist in the world of polarities. Every part within you that leans in one direction will create its opposite. This means that if you have a part that is very conservative, that wants your life to stay the same and does not like change, then you will also have the opposite part — a part that likes to do things spontaneously, to be free and make changes. You may find these two parts constantly playing against each other.

When you have two parts within you — one saying one thing and one saying the opposite — resolving these two sides allows your higher self to come through. One of the ways you can do this is to let the two parts carry on a dialogue. If you have a situation in your life in which you are going back and forth — with one part of you saying, "This is the answer; handle it this way," and another part saying, "No, it should be done *this* way" — then you can look at the situation as if the two parts were in conflict. Imagine one in each hand and create a dialogue between them. Let each express in turn what good it is trying to achieve, for each subpersonality is always trying to do something good for you, in the best way it knows how. Let the subpersonalities talk to each other and explore a compromise that would work for both. Show them mentally what you are trying to accomplish with your life and ask them to help you with your important goals.

Every single part of you has
a gift for you and is there
as your friend.

There is no voice within you that does not have the intent to help you. A voice or subpersonality that seems unhelpful may not have an accurate picture of what you want, or it may have been set up many years ago and is still operating from an old program. A part of you that experiences fear, for instance, may be trying to protect you from things it thinks might hurt you, even though you know now, from a higher level of understanding, that these same things cannot hurt you. Your journey in this lifetime is to bring all your parts up into your higher vision and purpose.

Learn to love each of your selves, for as you love them you begin the process of uniting them with your higher self.

Subpersonalities: Uniting the Separated Selves
PLAYSHEET

1. Take an area of your life in which you are experiencing a problem or in which you feel there is some lack or limitation.

2. Now, decide which *part* of you is creating this issue. Close your eyes and imagine what this part looks like. Is it young or old? How is it dressed? What expressions does it have on its face?

3. Thank this part of you for trying, in the best way it knows how, to do something good for you. Ask it what good thing it is trying to accomplish. For instance, if it is holding you back, it may be trying to protect you and keep you safe. There is always something good this part thinks it is accomplishing. What good things does this part think it is doing for you?

4. Ask this part if it would be willing to accomplish the same thing but in a different way, one that would contribute to your higher good and fit who you are now. You might ask that protective part to keep an eye on new ways to help you enter into a new challenge or adventure.

5. Look again at this part of yourself. Does it look older, wiser, or happier? Thank this part of you for being so willing to listen and help you with your higher goals.

Daily Joy Practice

Today, if you choose, you can move closer to the integration of all of your subpersonalities. Doing this allows you to better act, think, and feel as your higher self, thus feeling more balanced, peaceful, and loving. You can integrate your subpersonalities through identifying them as they appear, and then loving them.

Think of a part of yourself that you really like — a certain way of being, thinking, and acting. Infuse the subpersonality you like with waves of love and appreciation for all the good it is doing for you. Know that as you send it love and gratitude, you are aligning this subpersonality with your innermost being, your soul.

Now take a part of yourself, a subpersonality, that you do not like and have labeled as a wrong way to act or be. Perhaps this part of you is fearful, worried, or angry. Connect with the innermost part of your being and feel its unconditional love. Without judgment, with pure love, embrace this part of you. Thank it for trying in the best way it knows how to do something good for you. Offer this part of yourself understanding and compassion. Feel this part of you being drawn to the love you are offering, transforming it in some way. Know that as you do this you are unifying this subpersonality with your soul.

Today as you sense different aspects of your personality arising, stop for a moment and make contact with your soul. Feel its love, appreciation, and compassion reaching out to each of your subpersonalities, transforming them in some way. At the end of the day take a moment to reflect on how your day has been different or better in some way because of appreciating and loving all your subpersonalities.

AFFIRMATIONS

I love and appreciate all the parts of myself.

I know that all my subpersonalities are working for me
in the best way they know how.

I align all my subpersonalities
with my soul and spirit.

I align all my subpersonalities
with my goals and higher purpose.

I am on my higher path.

I recognize and listen when a part of me is
trying to get my attention.

CHAPTER EIGHT

Love: Knowing the Wisdom of the Heart

L ove is the food of the Universe. It is the most important ingredient in life. Children go toward love; they thrive on love and grow on love, and they would die without it. Love is an energy that circles the world; it exists everywhere and in everything. Every aspect of your life involves love. Even the darkest moment has within it an element of love — the need for it, the lack of it, or the desire to create more. So much of the energy on this planet is directed toward having love, and yet so many thoughtforms about love exist in every culture that make love hard to experience.

In speaking of love, I would like to speak of the common thoughts that exist about love. The thoughts people have about something are available to you telepathically, so when you are reaching for love, you are also pulling in the universal broadcast of it (along with all the mass beliefs that come with it).

Love can be expressed at the highest levels as a particle that is traveling so fast it is everywhere at once and becomes all there is, omnipresent. You could view love as an element that holds together the particles in an atom. It is a force like gravity or magnetism, but most people do not yet understand love as a force. All of you are striving for higher forms of love, but many of you get caught in the common thoughtforms that exist about it.

Imagine that there is a barrier to how much love you can absorb — such as the speed of light, which has an upper limit. It has been said that nothing is faster than the speed of light, yet there is, though it is not yet known in your Universe. It is the same with love, for on the earth plane there is a point of love that is the highest expression of love humanity as a whole has reached. Yet even more love is possible. All of your great masters and teachers are working with a medium, a dimension of love, to bring more love through to the earth plane. What would this love feel like? How would you know if you had it?

All of you have had an experience of that kind of love. You have words and terms about what love is, and yet you know love is more than words or thoughts. It is an experience, a knowing, a connection to another, to the earth, and ultimately to the higher self and soul. All people strive to deepen their relationship with their innermost, true self.

Often people offer you the opportunity
to know your higher and better self
through the platform of their love.

Sometimes it may seem as if, when you strive for higher expressions of love, the personality frequently comes in with its doubts, fears, and expectations. To have more love you will need to break through your past limitations around love. If you use the past to remember when your efforts at being loving did not work, you will re-create your past limitations in your present and future relationships. You can increase the love in your life by looking forward, letting go of your past patterns, and believing in your ability to love even more than you have ever loved in the past. Another way to have more love is to remember the times in which you were strong, loving, and full of light.

What does love bring up for most people? On a mass level, love brings up many pictures of form. In a relationship, it brings up commitment, marriage, ceremony, and ritual. In a family, it brings up taking care of others, being taken care of, dependence, and independence. It brings up attachment and detachment. On the personality level, love often brings up its opposite — fear. So many of you who have fallen in love or have had deep experiences of love find that, in response to feeling this much love, you retract or contract, pulling away from the other person or withdrawing your love.

The personality steps in and talks to you with its doubts and worries. You can deal with this by loving your personality and by reassuring it. Every time you open up to a new dimension of love, you always bring to the surface those parts of you that have felt unloved. You may transfer these fears to the other person, blaming him or her for pulling away, or you may create a situation that justifies not loving that person as much. Yet it is within you; it is *you* who creates the withdrawal. Rather than blame the other person when doubt, fear, or disappointment come up, look inward and ask, "Is a part of me creating a reason to be afraid?" Talk to that part. Reassure it that there is nothing wrong with that fear, and show it the new and bright future you are going toward.

Imagine there are many telepathic messages that exist on your planet, and that with each topic you think of, you tune in to all the other people who are thinking of the same thing. Now, if you are thinking of love, how loved you are, how much love there is in the Universe, how light and joyful you feel, then you will tap into all those other people who exist at that same frequency and strengthen your ability to love and be loved. When doubts and fears come up, they bring you into resonance with the thoughts and vibration of people who are living at that level of fear and can amplify your own fears. Do not make those types of thoughts wrong, but do not dwell on them, either. Do not spend time going over in your mind why something may not work, but instead focus on how it *can* work, how much love you can offer everyone — your children, your parents, your friends, and those you love deeply and closely.

Love transcends the self.

Most of you have had that experience of deep love in which you were able to set aside your personality, your own wants and desires, to assist another. Love is an energy you can tap into whenever you have a loving thought of anyone. You literally raise your own vibration. There are many high beings, such as myself and those who work at this level, who are focusing love on the planet, amplifying your feelings of love. Any time you express unconditional love, from your deepest being, and any time you receive it, you assist many more people in achieving it also.

Love from the higher realms is absolute compassion and complete detachment. It is seeing the larger picture of people's lives and focusing on, not what you want from them, but how you can assist them in their unfoldment and growth. Love is focusing on how you may serve them, and in doing so, how you may serve your own growth and higher purpose.

Love opens the door to your own growth and aliveness. You may have experienced how being in love expands your aliveness — being in love with anyone, be it a child, a parent, or a friend. The joy to me in coming through and assisting others is watching those I speak to grow and love themselves more. That energy comes back to me and is amplified many times, so that I in turn can assist even more people through my broadcast of love.

Think for a moment of today or tomorrow. What is your day like? Is there something you could do to give love to someone or to experience more love yourself?

Acknowledging people and acknowledging yourself is another way to experience love. Take a moment to appreciate everyone you see and to send them a feeling of love. This will change your life and raise your vibration rapidly. Being committed to the idea of love will bring it to you. Do not get into the personality level, where you ask, "Will this situation last, will it work?" Instead, ask right now, "How can I deepen the love that I have in this relationship?" Love operates in the present, and by focusing on it in the present, you send it into the future and release it to the past.

If you exist in a feeling of love —
if you can find it in everything you do,
transmit it through your touch,
through your words, eyes, and feelings —
you can cancel out with one act of love
thousands of acts of a lower nature.

You can help transform the planet. It does not take that many people focused on love to change the destiny of humankind, for love is one of the most powerful energies in the Universe. It is thousands of times stronger than anger, resentment, or fear.

For a moment, think of three people who could use your unconditional love, and send it to them. Imagine three people you would be willing to receive unconditional love from. Then, open to receive it.

Can you imagine how it would feel if your heart were open, if everywhere you went you trusted and knew that the Universe was friendly? How would your life flow if you believed that your inner guidance was gentle and kind and that people were sending you love wherever you went, and that you were broadcasting a beam of love to everyone? How would your life change if whenever someone said something to you, no matter how it came out, you could recognize the love or the need for love behind it? You would be constantly looking deeper to acknowledge and recognize the love within each person, as I do. By recognizing love, you draw it out of people and attract it to yourself wherever you go.

As you go out into the world today, be aware of how you can express love through your eyes, through your smile, your heart, and even a gentle touch if it is appropriate. You came to earth as a community of souls, and all of you can send out a high loving feeling, a thoughtform of love, and offer it to each other. For the rest of today, be in your heart. Experience the love that is you, and as you do, be open to receive from others the acknowledgment of the beautiful light and love within you.

Love: Knowing the Wisdom of the Heart
PLAYSHEET

1. Think of at least three times in the past when you felt a surge of loving feelings as you thought of or talked to someone, or gave him or her love.

2. Think of three people who could use your love right now. Recall those loving feelings from step 1 above. Send that love out to these three people.

3. Think of three ways someone gave you love that was unexpected.

4. Reflect on some way you could surprise and delight someone today or tomorrow with an expression of your love.

DAILY JOY PRACTICE

Start by aligning with your soul, opening to the essence of love within you. Allow your soul's love to flow into your body, emotions, and mind, raising your vibration as it does. Give permission to your soul to take down any walls around your heart so that the love within you can flow out to the world.

Imagine that you are symbolically walking through a door into a new dimension of love. Sense your heart becoming like a radiant sun, touching and lifting up all life around you with love.

Think of something you are doing today, and picture love flowing out from you to everyone involved, through your thoughts, actions, and words. You offer love that is accepting and kind, that sees the goodness in others, that helps them recognize it in themselves, and that asks for nothing in return.

Imagine for today that every situation that comes your way, every thought that comes into your mind, every person you meet is providing you an opportunity to experience and express more of the love within you. Everything that you come across today is being created for your benefit, brought to you by your soul to expand your ability to love yourself and others.

Today you can choose to experience more of the love that is all around you, everywhere you look. Feel it coming from the Universe, from other people, from strangers, loved ones, and friends; feel it coming from flowers, plants, animals, and the earth itself. As you experience all the love around you, feel love flowing out of you, embracing the world and all life with the love that you are.

AFFIRMATIONS

I experience the love the Universe has for me.

I recognize and receive all the love
the Universe is offering me.

I have loving thoughts of others.

I offer unconditional love to others.

I am open to receive love from others.

I am aware of the larger picture of people's lives.

I acknowledge and appreciate the good in people.

My heart is open. I trust in the goodness of the Universe.

I remember all the love and the goodness the
Universe has offered me when I think about the past.

I am increasing my ability to experience and
express love every day.

I freely give and receive love.

I support the success and happiness of everyone I know.

Everyone I know supports my success and happiness.

My heart is like a sun that nurtures all life with love.

I open to receive my soul's love often.

I live in a wonderful, nurturing environment.

I recognize love or the need for love
behind everything people say to me.
I always respond with love.

CHAPTER NINE

Opening to Receive

I magine, if you will, that you are a king, and your treasury is full. In fact, you have so much you do not know where to begin distributing the wealth. All of the people in your kingdom are walking around saying how poor they are, but when you offer them your money, they act as if they do not see you, or they wonder what is wrong with what you are offering.

I look out and see the storehouses all over — untapped, unused, and even unrecognized. You have heard the expression "heaven on earth." There is nothing that stops you from having it, except your ability to ask for and receive it. What are these storehouses? What things lie within them that we would love to pass out?

One is love. We do not measure growth as you do (career advancements, more money, and so on). We look to spiritual evolution, which includes joy, self-love, the ability to receive, reframing the negative into the positive, the refinement of the ego, a willingness to embrace the new, and the ability to work together for common purpose.

There is so much love available,
it is as abundant as the air you breathe.

Do you ask for love? The more you give and receive
love, the greater your spiritual growth. Every moment you
spend focused on something that is not working, thinking of
someone who does not love you, makes you like the people
who turn away from the king's treasure. You always have the
opportunity to think of times you felt loved, to imagine a
future of abundance, and thus to partake of spiritual wealth.

What do you think of? Every in-breath takes you up to the
world of essence where form is created, and on the out-breath
you send to the world your wishes. Every time you recognize
the love you have, you increase it. One of the laws of receiving
is that recognizing when you have gotten something increases
it in your life, and every time you do not acknowledge something you make it so much harder to have more sent to you.

The more you focus on what is wrong, the more wrong you
will create in your life, and the more it will spread to areas that
were working. The more you concentrate on what is right in
your life, on what is working, the more other areas of your life
will work. It is the same in receiving. The more you acknowledge how much you are receiving, the more you will have.

There are two kinds of requests: those made by your
personality, and those made by your soul.

What are the requests
of your soul?

A request for spiritual evolution is a soul request, as is a
request for higher purpose, clarity, love, and focus. A desire

to find your higher path or for more light in your life is also a soul request.

Personality requests can have the clothing of a soul request. They are usually more specific, such as a request for a new car or a material object, for instance. If you are willing to look at the deeper motivation behind what you want, and what you expect to get from having it, then you will open up many more ways and forms in which your request can come to you.

A personality request is very specific, so it often takes longer for the Universe to find ways to get it to you. If, however, instead of asking for money, you ask for what the money would bring you — such as more security or the ability to travel, to take time off from your job, or to pay your bills every month with ease — the Universe and your soul can bring these to you more easily.

Learning to receive is learning to ask for the essence of what you want, rather than the form.

Often the Universe brings what you specifically ask for, and you find it is not what you want. This wastes much time. Before you say that you want something, ask, "Is there any broader or more accurate way I can state that request?"

When you say, "I want this man or woman to love me" or "I want this person to bring me joy," then you have made it very difficult for the Universe to give you what you want, especially if that person does not love you or bring you joy. If instead you say, "I am open to receiving love from a man or woman who will love me," then it is much easier to have it, for you are not attached to the form (a specific person) but rather to the essence (love and joy).

If you want something to appear in a specific way, it may take longer than if you let the Universe create magic and miracles and bring you the soul request, rather than the personality desire. Often, this requires the ability to let go and detach.

You may have experienced picturing something and having it come to you. Yet many of you do not know how to let go of the old and open to the new. Be willing to be open to new forms if you want to receive.

If you are cluttering your life with many relationships, for instance, or if you are filling your time with an unsatisfying relationship, then there is no room left in your life for a fulfilling one. If you are asking for more money but you are spending all your time giving away your services, or pursuing activities that do not bring you money, it will be much more difficult to attract it.

> *Be willing to do what your soul directs*
> *you to do if you want to create*
> *what you are asking for.*

Often when you ask for something, you will find yourself going through unexpected changes to prepare yourself for having it. Your attitude may need to change, or the viewpoint you are holding may be creating an energy block that is keeping you from having what you asked for. The Universe will immediately send you many experiences to open up and change your attitude, so that you can have what you requested.

Sometimes you must let go of certain things to have what you have asked for. You may need to release a thought, friend, useless activity, or a high level of worry. It is not that the Universe is punishing you, or trying to make it hard for you to get what you want, but that you have a gentle and loving inner teacher that wants to give things to you only when you are ready and it will be for your highest good.

Your innermost self and the Universe may not make a lot of money available to you, for instance, if you are not ready to handle it and it would not be for your higher good. Your higher self may bring you many lessons to change and shift your attitudes before money comes, so that it will truly benefit your growth. Many requests for fame and great amounts of money are not actually to your benefit, so your soul may slow down the arrival of these things, while it brings you other opportunities that are more appropriate for you, and while it strengthens you and builds a foundation for you to have these things.

You ask for so little, and that is what saddens us as we look over the minds of humanity. We see the limited focus of your thoughts, looking so close at hand rather than reaching for the heights.

There are ways to have more in your life.

One way to have more in your life is to use your imagination, for it is a great gift the Universe has given you. Every time you imagine having something, challenge yourself — imagine having even more! If you want a house, a friend, a lover or any relationship, a car, a life of leisure — fantasize about it and enlarge the vision.

Fantasy can lead to higher purpose. For many of the things you fantasize about the most (even those you feel furthest from having) can be pictures of your higher purpose and the life you will lead as you reach it.

What can you ask for? You can ask for spiritual evolution and more light, for that is a general request that your soul will utilize to bring you many unexpected gifts. (You will want to acknowledge these gifts when they come.)

Trust yourself and believe you can create what you want.

Having faith in yourself, and letting go of memories when things did not work, will help you open to more abundance. If you must think of the past, think of those times you were powerful and creative. Go into your heart and ask whether you feel you deserve all the joy and love that is awaiting you on your path of higher purpose.

You can begin to imagine joy, peace, and harmony as your birthright. Focus, clarity, and love are available for the asking. Request a vision of your higher purpose, and be willing to recognize the gifts every day as they come, even the small things. The more you acknowledge what the Universe is sending you, the more you can bring into your life.

Ask! We cannot give you anything unless you ask. The Universe waits for you to ask. When you see it coming, be willing to take and receive it. When the opportunity comes, grab it! Thank and acknowledge the Universe for it, and you can create heaven on earth.

Opening to Receive

PLAYSHEET

1. Think of at least four things in your life you are doing well, things that are working and that you feel good about.

2. What good things have you received from the Universe in the last week or month? Can you come up with at least ten things?

3. Think of at least five things you asked for in the past and received.

4. What would you like to receive from the Universe right now? Use your imagination and ask for all you can think of. Example: I am open to receiving all of the resources I need to create my higher purpose.

DAILY JOY PRACTICE

You can receive so much more than you may have thought to ask for. Asking for spiritual qualities and spiritual evolution will lift you higher and make it easier to have everything else in your life you have been wanting. You can ask for more light, joy, peace, clarity, love, wisdom, vision, and to find and follow your higher path.

Take a moment to request from your soul whatever spiritual quality you would like to experience more of. Set your intention to receive this from your innermost self right now. Know that your soul always responds, and it will give you whatever you ask for that is for your higher good. Picture yourself demonstrating this quality throughout the day, and imagine how your day will be different as you do.

Take time at the end of the day to reflect on your day. Did you experience and demonstrate this quality, even if just once or for just a moment? Acknowledge every moment this quality came into your mind, and every time you were able to experience it. Even if you only remembered to experience this quality for a short moment, give yourself credit for receiving what you asked for. You might ask your innermost self to increase your ability to demonstrate this quality even more over the next few days. Be sure to acknowledge your ability to receive every time you experience this quality.

Open to receive all the good the Universe is bringing you in every moment. It might come in the form of clarity, hope, inspiration, or in a thousand other ways. Affirm that you trust that the Universe is always working for you and with you, even if it does not seem so. Thank and appreciate the Universe for all the good that is coming to you today and in every day of your life.

AFFIRMATIONS

I open to receive more love, joy, and abundance.

I open to receive and express greater clarity,
wisdom, and understanding.

I ask for and experience an increase in my spiritual vision.

I ask for and receive assistance to find and
follow my higher path.

I open to receive the gifts of consciousness
my soul has for me.

I open to receive love and to recognize love
in all of its forms.

I acknowledge often how much I receive
from the Universe.

I open to receive what I ask for
in its highest and best form.

I open to receive what I want in whatever timing is
best for my higher good.

I ask for and receive my higher good in every area of my life.

I release all obstacles to receiving my higher good.

I receive every gift the Universe has for me.

I appreciate and acknowledge all that I have.
I live an abundant life.

I deserve love and I open to receive it.

I deserve joy and I open to receive it.

I deserve the best possible life and I have it.

I am creating heaven on earth.

CHAPTER TEN

Appreciation, Gratitude, and the Law of Increase

I f you want to come out of a bad space, if you are drained or depleted, if you have been around someone who upset you, then you can quickly change your energy by looking at the good things you have and saying thanks — thank you *self*, thank you *Universe*. This is an effective way of purifying your aura and raising your vibration. If you were to wake up each morning and spend two minutes giving thanks, you would find yourself having a much higher day.

What is the purpose of gratitude? It is not just something you have to do because your parents told you to say thank you and be polite. You have heard of people who give thanks after coming through an ordeal. There is a higher reason for gratitude and thanks. Gratitude literally sends out a call to the Universe to give you more.

Whatever you appreciate and give thanks for will increase in your life.

Have you ever noticed how much you like to be with people who thank you, who appreciate and acknowledge you? When you give them advice, they say, "Thank you, that helps so much." When you offer them something, they hold it and love it. Have you noticed how you want to give them more? It is the same, on an energy level, with the Universe. Whenever you stop to thank the Universe for the abundance you have, the Universe will give you more. Whenever you give thanks, you increase the light in your aura at that very moment. You change it through your heart, for the feeling of gratitude comes from the heart. As you give thanks, you open your heart. Your heart is the door to your soul; it is the link between the world of form and the world of essence. Gratitude and thanks are a path straight to the heart, to your essence and your soul.

You can purify your aura and raise your vibration by giving thanks. The resonance of gratitude in your body vibrates with your heart center. It allows you to open to receive more. It opens your heart and heals the physical body with its radiance of love. It sets up a higher, finer vibration, and it is your vibration that makes you magnetic to love and all good things. When you give thanks, the Universe sets up a matching note or sound that brings you even more of the same.

There are various methods of expressing thanks — mental, verbal, and written. An emotional, heartfelt sense of gratitude is the most important. No matter how you give thanks, if you do so idly, without paying attention and feeling it in your heart, then it is not as effective as when you are fully aware and coming from true gratitude. When you *think* "thank you," it has an effect on your body, yet it is even more powerful to say it aloud. Have you been around people who constantly thank you? I am not speaking of those who do it from habit or because they are always apologizing or wanting your favor.

I am referring to people who truly acknowledge and appreciate you when you are with them. These people are increasing what they will receive from other people and from the world.

The process of writing ideas down and speaking them puts them out into the world of form more quickly than just thinking them. If you want something, write it down or say it aloud, because the processes of speech and writing are one step closer to having something than the process of thinking. The hands and the throat are two centers of manifestation. The ideas in your mind, when expressed to others, become part of the world of form. When written on paper, they are even closer to being created. It is all right to express thanks in your mind. That will evolve you also, but it is even more powerful to say it aloud to the Universe and to others.

To create something new, or to keep receiving more of something you already have, get some paper and pens and write a thank-you to the Universe.

At night, make a list of everything you received during the day. It may be something you bought, a smile from a stranger, a good feeling or extra energy, a car that got you where you wanted to go, or money. You will be amazed at all the gifts that the Universe sends your way every day. By acknowledging what you receive, you create a connection with the Universe that will allow you to have even more.

You may want to write or call someone who has helped you and express your appreciation. The more you express outwardly your gratitude and thankfulness for what you have, the more you change your molecular vibration away from the dense energy and into finer levels. You may notice that highly evolved souls and great teachers spend much of their time appreciating and thanking the Universe. In their meditation they feel true humility and gratitude for everything they are given.

What is the effect of gratitude on the various bodies? The physical body literally undergoes a change when you are appreciative. When you acknowledge your good health, for instance, you send a message to the cells in your body. They respond to it, for each of your cells has within it the hologram of the whole of you. Each cell has its own awareness. (Not that they think in the same way you do.) You are composed of many different cells that function at a level of awareness that is not the same as the overall awareness you call "I." They like you to appreciate them also. If you want to heal a problem in your body, instead of remembering those times when you were not healthy, or worrying about future pains or problems, thank your body for all the wonderful things it is doing well. If you send it gratitude frequently, you will find it doing even more for you. The cells definitely understand the feeling of gratitude and will try to work for you even harder.

Express appreciation for how well your body moves, acts, and gets you around. Appreciate how it converts your food into energy and how well it serves you. On the other hand, if you look at your body and make it wrong, saying, "I do not like my thighs, my stomach," and so on, if you complain about it, you will find that it does not respond as well. Think of your body as containing millions of little entities — cells — that have feelings. The minute you make up your mind to appreciate them, you change your physical vibration. The cells immediately go to work to increase your energy. When you have a negative thought, one of ingratitude, then your energy drops.

Gratitude is healing to the emotions.

Gratitude links the emotional body to the heart and thus to the soul, which is reached through the heart. The emotional body is a restless, constantly vibrating flow of energy around you. When you say thanks, and appreciate your life, acknowledging people, events, and the higher forces, the pattern of energy that represents your emotional body begins to rearrange itself into a higher and finer vibration. Your emotions are the most magnetic part of you when it comes to attracting events, people, and objects. The calmer and more detached you are, the easier it is to have what you want. You need to direct your will and intent toward this goal. The more peaceful and serene you are, the more easily you can focus on your higher being and the more you can have.

When you experience emotionally a sense of deep gratitude, it is calming and effective in raising the vibration of your emotional body. The heart is most affected and most easily reached by gratitude. If you want to link with another person in your heart, appreciate him or her. By sending out your telepathic appreciation, you will automatically stop power struggles. When you see friends this week, notice and acknowledge something good about them. Be sure it is heartfelt and not something you have to make up. If you can find something to say to them that expresses gratitude for who they are, you will immediately move the level of contact up into the heart.

Giving thanks and appreciation
opens many doors into the
higher levels of the Universe.

Appreciation is a doorway into the heart. It opens your heart and allows you to experience more love in your life. Today and in the following days, when you remember to do so, appreciate each person you come in contact with or think about. If it is your friend or a loved one, a stranger or coworker, see if you can send him or her gratitude and thanks. Appreciate something about that person from your heart.

Gratitude takes you out of your head and judgment. Many of you are wrapped up in your thoughts, and when you give thanks, it takes you out of that mental place of right and wrong, good and bad, and puts you into your heart. When you get out of your mind level, even for a short time, it is possible for the Universe to work more directly with you. Often the level of mental activity going on in many of you creates so much confusion it is harder for you to get what you want.

When appreciation is felt in the mental body (the part of you that thinks all the time), it literally silences your doubting, worrying, or skeptical side. It brings together all your selves under a new banner, and it can be a doorway into a new level of energy. Whenever you find yourself upset or concerned, experiencing something that does not feel healing, stop and give thanks for the good things you have.

A feeling of gratitude allows you access to your abstract mind, which is the part of you that links the right and left brain, the male and female sides. The abstract mind not only works with the left-brain side, which deals with numbers, figures, and logic, but it also works with the right-brain side, which deals with creativity, intuition, and feelings. It synthesizes these two parts. The union comes when you are able to conceptualize frameworks of beliefs and realities that are outside your normal way of thinking. This feels like light coming through in the form of a new solution to an old problem, an inspiration, or a revelation.

The abstract mind is able to see the larger picture of your life. This part of you has many new ways of thinking; it exists beyond the normal framework you live in. The abstract mind does not think in terms you are used to. It is the genius level that exists within all of you. It is the highest form of thinking you have, and if you use this type of thinking often, it can greatly assist you in evolving.

You can choose to think in a higher way more often.

Giving thanks will lead you directly to your heart and your abstract mind. By giving thanks, you bring light into your crown center at the top of your head, through the doorway of your heart. Because of the increased light and new heart opening, your innermost self and the Universe can send you many ideas and gifts. These gifts may unfold in a week, or a month, but you have created an opening for many good things to come to you. Imagine that gratefulness allows you to reach into and change your vibration, to go to the higher levels of wisdom that are available in the Universe. The Universe definitely hears and appreciates your thank-yous, and you will be sent energy back.

All of you have desires, and desires make up what I call your "desire body." There are things that you want to have in your life. If I asked you what you desire, what is most important to have right now, you could tell me if you stopped and thought about it. When you give thanks, you affect your desire body. The desire body is quite restless, like the emotional body. It is always focusing on what it does not have and what it wants to create. It has a purpose, for it brings you new forms, motivation, and creative energy. Yet it can bring you a sense of runaway energy — reminding you of all the things you have yet to do and create.

Your desires can seem overwhelming, if you have too many unfulfilled ones. Giving thanks directly affects desires by allowing them to calm down and to see how much they have created. Think of it as if you have a separate part of you composed of those things you have been wanting. When you give thanks, it empowers this part. This part of you does not usually focus on what you have generated, but it wants to tell you what you could do, how much harder you could work, and on and on. It always has lists of things for you to do, and it needs you to reassure it, to talk to it and calm it down. Feeling appreciation for what you have done will accomplish this, and it will strengthen this part in its ability to create more.

Another body is that of the personal will. All of you have different pictures of this will. Some of you call it "willpower."

Will is the ability to direct your energy where you want it to go.

Many of you want to go higher, into the finer levels of energy where there is more peace, joy, contentment, and detachment. Higher Will is like a stream or river of energy that moves through you all the time. When you give thanks, you strengthen your higher Will. Not willpower, but Will that is linked with the heart, Will that is directed to doing what you love. The more you appreciate yourself, acknowledge everything in your life, the more you link your heart with higher Will. This allows you to create those things your heart has been wanting.

Appreciation, Gratitude, and the Law of Increase

PLAYSHEET

1. What things do you appreciate having in your life right now?

2. What people do you appreciate?

3. What good things about yourself — your body, your mind, and so on — do you appreciate?

4. Now express your appreciation. Call someone on the phone or write and express your appreciation of him or her.

Daily Joy Practice

Take a moment to feel the love in your heart and acknowledge what a loving person you are. Appreciate yourself right now for all the goodness, kindness, good intentions, and love that you offer the world and everyone around you. Forgive yourself for moments when you were not as high and loving as you would like to be. Ask your soul to increase your ability to appreciate all that you are and all that you have so that you can focus on what is working well in your life rather than on what seems to need improving.

Think of your day ahead, and imagine what the day might be like if you acknowledged everything about your life that you appreciate. How might you feel if you expressed gratitude to the Universe for everything you have? How might your relationships with other people change if you took time to appreciate them today, either through your thoughts and feelings or through taking outer action?

Picture yourself going about your day, expressing goodwill, kindness, and appreciation for every person and situation in your life. Imagine appreciating all the abundance that you have and acknowledging everything that is working well. See yourself expressing gratitude often throughout the day, both gratitude to the Universe and gratitude to other people for everything you can think of. As you send out your appreciation and gratitude, the Universe and other people will send you energy back, although you are not sending out gratitude for this purpose. Know that whatever you focus on will increase.

AFFIRMATIONS

I focus on what is working in my life.
As I do, I draw even more good things into my life.

I offer appreciation to everyone I know.

I am grateful for the wonderful life I have.

I am grateful for _____.
(Finish the sentence.)

I see and acknowledge the goodness in others.

I thank the Universe for all the abundance I have.

I am grateful for all the love I have in my life.

I say thank you often.

I appreciate my family and friends.

I appreciate and support people for who they are.

Everyone appreciates and supports me for who I am.

I find new things to be grateful for every day.

I release my past by appreciating that everything
I did got me to where I am now.

I accept my higher good in every area of my life.

I focus on what is good and loving in other people,
thus contributing to their ability to experience
themselves in a more positive way.

I consciously offer light to everyone I am with.

I speak positive, uplifting words.

I love my body. I send it thanks for all the
good things it does for me.

CHAPTER ELEVEN

Feeling Inner Peace

W hat is inner peace? All of you have a picture in your mind of what you think inner peace is. You have achieved this state many times, sometimes for moments, even for hours, and so you know what inner peace feels like. Part of growth is learning to create that feeling without being dependent upon things turning out a certain way or needing people to respond in a specific way. You want to create inner peace as something you are and be able to give and share it with others. *You* become the center, radiating your soul's light outward, rather than reacting, or waiting for situations, relationships, and events in your life to be arranged in such a way that you have peace.

Creating inner peace from the higher levels is learning to open your heart. It means that you are not focused or attached on an emotional level to things that happen in the world around you. You know who you are, and you let things flow around you without touching or affecting your sense of peace.

You can learn to touch and affect the energy in the outer world from that center of energy within yourself. That is peace.

Opening the heart means remaining open and loving no matter what another person does, no matter what occurs to you, or what happens in your career. It means choosing to feel peaceful no matter what your outer life looks like. It is easy to be loving and open when those around you are loving; the challenge is to be loving when those around you are closed, afraid, or negative.

*Inner peace comes from within,
not from without.*

Anything you are attached to or must have a certain way, any belief or concept that is inflexible, will be an area in which your inner peace can be affected. The goal is to take that sense of inner peace and affect everything in the outer world, touching it with that energy. The first step is to *find* that sense of inner peace.

One of the simplest ways is through relaxing your body, which you can do both through physical touch and through mental relaxation. Your body can be the receptacle of many thoughts that are not peaceful. If you can bring your body to a state of peace and rest, the mind can be taught that feeling and learn to create it. Peace is more than just a feeling of relaxation in the body. It is a very specific radio wave, a vibration you send out that affects everything in your outer world.

You can begin to experience various levels of inner peace, down to the deepest feelings of it. Start by finding a sense of peace within. Give yourself one opportunity in the next week to feel inner peace. You may want to create a place of beauty, a sense of timelessness, to play music — anything that helps you truly experience what peace means to you. From that space, from that knowing, you can begin to change everything you see in the outer world.

What is the value of inner peace? It certainly feels better to the emotional body. However, it is more than that — it is the ability to affect the outer world from your highest level, to create and manifest from a focused place of purpose and an inner sense of who you are. When you are tranquil and calm, when you slow down and feel relaxed, you are able to create and think at your higher levels. What you bring to earth and create from this space is your higher good.

You can create things when you feel tense, anxious, or fearful, but those things may not be for your highest good; in fact, they will probably not be. If, before you plan your life or think of new ideas, you find a sense of inner peace and operate from it, you will find your plans reflecting more of your soul's purpose than your personality's desires. If, before you act or speak, you bring in this sense of peace, you will find your world changing rapidly into a very different place.

*Inner peace is a connection
to your deeper self,
and it will assist you
in letting go of fear.*

Fear is a lower energy, a vibration of less light, and you can change it with love. One of the goals of having inner peace is healing fear. It may be a fear that someone will hurt or reject you, abandon or run away from you. It may be a fear that you cannot make it in the world, a fear of putting yourself out there and failing. Inner peace is a connection to the heart and a willingness to let go of fear. You can achieve inner peace by letting go of feeling you have to defend yourself, and by being willing to be vulnerable. It is not putting on an act for other people; it is being willing to shine through as who you are and knowing you are all right.

Having inner peace means committing to letting go of self-criticism and self-doubt. Everything other people say to you about yourself is a reflection of a voice within you. If you find people critical, first ask, is there a part of you that is criticizing yourself? As you let go of self-criticism, you will experience less criticism from others. Remember also that what people say to you is a reflection of who they are, how they perceive the world, and how they speak to themselves. They may criticize you because they are critical of themselves. See their actions and words as a statement of their beliefs and learn to remain calm and centered.

Inner peace heals. You do not need to focus on your fears in order to let go of them. By achieving a feeling of inner peace, holding any situation in your life up to the light, you will find your mind opening to new ideas, solutions, and answers that come from your soul. Inner peace is the connection to your spiritual self. You achieve it through physical relaxation in the body, emotional calm, and mental focus on higher ideals and qualities. If you wish to go upward, to experience and live in the higher levels of energy, inner peace is the doorway.

Once you decide to create inner peace, you may find many things happening that challenge your resolve to remain peaceful. You may say, "I can remain peaceful *except* if *this* or *that* happens." The Universe is sending you those exceptions as an opportunity to create a new response of peace instead of being upset.

How do you manifest inner peace and hold it steadily? You begin by acknowledging those moments when you have inner peace, attuning your awareness to the feeling, and by having the will and intent to create it. You can use your imagination to think of what it would feel like. You can think about or contemplate inner peace, for wherever you place your thoughts you begin to create your experience.

*You can decide
to stop being affected by
the outer world and, instead,
to affect the world around you
with your peace.*

No matter what happens each day, if unexpected bills arrive in the mail or someone changes his or her mind, no matter what in the past has destroyed your emotional calm, mental peace, or physical well-being, decide that you will now radiate peace, healing, and love. The world you see around you is but an illusion created by the energy you are sending out. Anything is possible. The limits you see — the part of you that says, "This cannot be done" — are only thoughts. You can absolutely change them. From a position of inner peace you can create the reflection of your soul's light in the outer world.

Manifesting inner peace means acting rather than reacting. It is a stance, an attitude; it is the energy you send outward into the world. It means you can connect with the Universe at your higher soul levels. Imagine there are many streams of energy around you, and you can choose to operate in any one you wish. You can choose one called *struggle* that involves a great deal of work to get what you want. You can also choose another stream of energy called *joy*. When you are anxious, tense, and worried, you are in the first stream. If for even a moment you find inner peace, you automatically join the second, higher flow of energy, that of joy.

There are many people alive right now who are creating and experiencing energy flows of creativity, peace, and light. Whenever you achieve inner peace, you link with all those beings who are living in and creating this higher energy flow. Ideas may begin to come to you. You can pull in anything you need from this position of peace.

To have inner peace, you need to be willing to open your heart. When something happens that would normally make you feel defensive or closed, when you would normally pull away or choose to feel hurt, you have another choice. If instead you are willing to open your heart just one more notch, to experience a little more compassion and understanding for other people, you will find yourself able to send them love and create a feeling of peace for yourself.

You can choose to see
the world any way
you want.

You may say, "Yes, but this is the way my life is. These are the facts. If only this situation changed, or I had more money, or this person would stop irritating me, I could discover inner peace." What you experience as real is simply a reflection of your belief systems and your mind. If you choose to experience inner peace anyway, you can change everything you now experience as real — bringing in new ideas and beliefs that might work in higher and better ways.

Forgiveness is necessary for inner peace. If there are people from your past you hold a grudge against, or feel negatively toward, you can in a few minutes forgive them and let go. If someone has not returned your call or letter, owes you something, or has hurt you badly, you will clear your own energy if you forgive, let go, and detach. Inner peace means releasing attachments to anything — whether to having a person act the way you want or to having the world work the way you expect. When you let go of those attachments, you will find your life working even better than you could have expected or planned. It does not mean giving up control of your life; it means coming from your own center of peace at all times.

Inner peace also means forgiving yourself. Remember to love yourself, knowing that you are a good person, always doing the best you know how and are capable of doing in each moment. When you can forgive yourself, it is easier to forgive other people, knowing that they, too, are doing the best they know how and are able to do at this time.

Right now, make the decision to bring inner peace into your life. Make the decision to open your heart even more, to be more compassionate, more understanding, more loving, and more forgiving of everyone you know, including yourself. Form a picture in your mind of yourself going through the next week, and see yourself coming from a totally new level of peace. See the smile on your face, the peace in your mind, and the joy in your heart.

Take one thing in your life that you would like to feel peace about, something that possibly you have been reacting to, and imagine releasing, forgiving, and letting go, thus finding inner peace with this issue. Only you can create inner peace. From that space, you will see the world you experience reflecting it. Other people, events, and situations do not need to trigger a reaction in you. If, instead, you maintain this center of peace, you will change those events that used to disturb and upset you. If they do not change, it will no longer intrude on your sense of well-being. You can find your center, your soul's light, and your inner being reflected and carried out in the world you experience.

Feeling Inner Peace

PLAYSHEET

Relax your body. Take three deep breaths and let all tension go.

1. Remember three times when you felt inner peace. Really experience that peaceful feeling.

2. What things take away your peaceful feeling? For each, finish this sentence: I can be peaceful except when _____. (For example, "except when someone around me is in a bad mood.")

3. Say to yourself, "The part of me that does not feel peaceful is only a small part, and I now identify and connect with my strong inner self. This strong side is now putting more light into that small fearful part."

4. Now take every statement above and turn it into a positive affirmation. For example: "My strong inner self feels peace even when someone around me is in a bad mood." As you do so, let yourself feel the strength of your wise, confident self, and then release, forgive, and let go of each situation that is a distraction to your inner peace.

DAILY JOY PRACTICE

As you think about the day ahead, connect with your soul, and ask to feel more of the deep, abiding peace of your innermost self. Grow quiet for a moment, relax your body, and affirm that you are open to experience more inner peace right now and throughout the day.

Allow the peace of your innermost self to permeate your mind, allowing you to have a quieter mind and more peaceful thoughts. Feel this deep peace calming your emotions. Let this peace flow into your body, allowing your muscles to unwind and feel more relaxed. Notice how much more peaceful, centered, and balanced you now feel. Note how your peaceful thoughts, calm emotions, and relaxed body enhance the feeling that all is well with the world.

Let someone, or several people, come to mind while you are in this state of peace. Radiate the peace you are feeling to whoever comes to mind right now. Sense how it feels to radiate peace to others.

Picture yourself going through the day in this peaceful, centered, and balanced state. Think of the people you will be with today. Imagine yourself feeling peaceful around everyone, offering your peace to others in this way. Observe how you feel about people and how they respond when you are in this state. Say to yourself, "I choose peace. I offer my peace to the world and all life in it."

AFFIRMATIONS

My thoughts are peaceful.

My emotions are calm and flowing.

My body is relaxed.

I feel balanced and centered.

I stay in my calm, peaceful center no matter
what is happening around me.

I create from a peaceful inner state
that brings me my highest good.

I speak to others from a place of inner peace.

My inner peace connects me to my soul,
my innermost being.

My inner peace opens the door to higher energy.

My inner peace brings me answers, ideas, and solutions.

I stay in my center, radiating peace and love.

My inner peace creates a new, higher reality for me.

I experience inner peace by forgiving and letting go.

I come from my center of peace at all times.

I acknowledge the many times I have chosen peace
in the past.

I am a peaceful person.

I maintain my inner peace around other people.

I join a higher flow of energy as I choose inner peace.

My peace allows me to affect the world
around me from my highest level.

I positively affect everyone around me with my peace.

I am peaceful. I choose peace.

CHAPTER TWELVE

Achieving Balance, Stability, and Security

Y ou can create stability by calming down and taking a few moments to think before you act. Continuous action without pause is appropriate for some of the tasks you have to do and inappropriate if done all the time.

As you move through the day, many of you engage in continuous motion, going from one thing to the next as each comes across your mind or catches your eye. If you wish to feel stable and balanced, stop often throughout the day and focus on what you are doing. Change your perspective. Sit quietly and experience yourself and your thoughts from a calmer level of awareness. This involves bringing your emotions into a state of peace and quiet. When you change your position and sit down, putting your hands at your sides, your breathing changes. When there is no motion in your body other than your thoughts, you can think in a different way.

You may experience a greater connection to your higher self at this time. As you pause for a moment in your daily activities, resting your body, quieting your mind, and calming your emotions, you will discover many new ways to look at what is happening in your life. When you are continuously in motion, you think differently from when you sit down and get quiet. Quieting your physical body enables your spirit to come into your thoughts, particularly as you become peaceful and serene.

You can achieve balance and stability by checking with your higher self before taking action, especially on important issues. That means giving yourself the opportunity to view things from many different angles before acting. It means allowing yourself to take whatever time is necessary to do a good job. You can avoid many things that take you off balance by giving yourself enough time to think before you act. There is a saying, "Look before you leap." You do not need to stop before every action you take, but you can make your life much easier and more joyful if you stop and think about something important before you take action or before you speak to someone about an important issue. It may be the purchasing of a new car or the signing of a contract. All changes can bring balance and peace when viewed with careful thought. If you are in continuous motion, you can end up making decisions and taking actions that lead to crisis and problems.

If you have a decision to make about something you consider important, do not rush into it. As you allow yourself time to think about it, you live out many probable futures in your mind, and you begin to see the consequences of certain actions. One of the gifts of your world is that it is a place of action and reaction. Whenever you take an action, you set ripples into motion, like the ripples on a pond when you throw in a stone. Every action affects probable futures and makes changes in your life path. The more you can anticipate what things might be affected by your actions and take action from that perspective of greater wisdom, the more you will create joy and balance in your future.

Your attitude determines how you experience the world.

Your attitude is the way you react to things that happen in your life. An attitude that creates joy is one in which you interpret what happens to you through the filter of joy. Your attitude and outlook act like a filter. When you have a positive, optimistic outlook, it filters out negative and denser perspectives and leads to joy.

Your attitude is reflected in the words you use when you talk to yourself. Perhaps you have just succeeded in achieving a goal you wanted to accomplish. A joyful attitude says, "Congratulations, job well done." If your joyful self speaks words of praise, it helps you bring more of the same to yourself. Attitudes are magnetic, and every moment you spend in joy magnetizes another moment of joy. Joyful, light emotions are always more powerful in their ability to create than negative emotions.

Stability comes from an attitude of balance. When things happen to you, your response to them creates your inner balance. If a friend is having problems and you respond by feeling angry or sad, you have moved away from your own center and allowed your friend's energy to affect you.

As you create more balance and stability in your life, you will be able to observe when you have let other people's problems affect you. It is most noticeable when those problems have no impact on your life, do not affect you directly, and yet you are still depressed or upset. Observe those situations in which your balance is disturbed by another's lack of balance.

The next step is to tell yourself that you can keep your balance, that you are not dependent upon others acting or responding in a balanced way for you to remain centered and balanced.

Many of you allow yourselves to respond in an unstable or insecure way when someone around you is acting that way. When someone is speaking to you about something you did wrong, or accusing you of something, instead of feeling angry, you can choose to keep your sense of balance even though the other person is not able to do so. As his or her energy comes into you and you begin to feel it unbalancing you, see that you are resonating with that unbalanced part in the other person. To stop responding in this way, send this person love. As you do, you reassert your own balance and connect with your higher self.

Balance is finding the midway point between opposites. You are always involved in maintaining balance, both literally in the mechanism of the inner ear and symbolically through the juggling of all the things in your life. Whatever you picture balance to be, it will be.

*You create balance by visualizing balance,
and by being clear that those pictures
of balance are what you want.*

Some of you define balance as boring, for you thrive on things being slightly out of balance, creating drama and intense emotions. You have seen people whose lives are in constant upset, who go from one crisis to another. What they picture as balance is moving back and forth between extremes.

To some the thought of balance and stability means a void of emotions, something that can seem frightening. As you reach higher levels of consciousness, your emotions become so calm they are like the still lake that reflects the sun. Many people, however, fear having no emotions, and they will create anything to get attention rather than have no attention paid to them at all. Often people create upset and problems all around them because they are afraid that, if everything were calm, no one would pay attention to them or life would be boring. They would rather have negative attention than no attention at all.

Some of you depend on intense emotions to feel alive. Yet intense, dramatic emotions always take you away from your center. Some of you, when you are feeling very peaceful, having little emotion, think you are sad or depressed. Whenever you get silent within, do you begin to think that something is wrong? Are you addicted to strong, intense emotions? Do you feel good when things are peaceful and calm, or do you begin to worry about what will go wrong next? It takes patience to get used to being calm. Although you might think it would be easy, it is harder for most people to adapt to a peaceful environment than to a disruptive one. If the environment is too peaceful, many will create turbulence because it is what they are used to.

People need different things to maintain their balance. Some people need a steady job, some require large blocks of time off, and others need much activity and constant variety. Go within for a moment and picture a time in your life when you felt stable and balanced. If you cannot think of a time, think of a symbol to represent that balance you would like in your life. Now picture yourself feeling balanced in the future. Having a symbol to represent something is a very powerful way to draw it to you. Symbols work on a deeper level of consciousness than words and bypass belief systems.

Balance is about moderation, not extremes. Maintaining balance in your life means doing the right amount of each thing. Some of you think that things would be better if you only had more time off. Yet, when people retire, they find that there is such a thing as too much time off. There is a balance between work and play, sleep and wakefulness, time together and time apart that will create the most peace and joy for you. You do not create balance by eliminating opposites. Balance is doing things in moderation, stopping when the energy is gone and riding the waves as they come in. It means pacing yourself in a steady, even way.

Some of you keep going long after the energy to do something has left. Do those things that bring you aliveness. There is a proper mix of focus and daydreaming, intellect and intuition, sitting and movement that brings joy. Most of you need variety, and everyone needs to keep growing. Balance is finding the proper mix of activities that support your aliveness and allow you to joyfully accomplish your purpose.

Some people feel balanced when they feel peaceful; others feel balanced when they create excitement, when things are moving rapidly in their lives and they are busy juggling many things. Some picture balance as things going well and being under control. You are constantly creating the degree of balance you will have in the future by how you picture yourself in the future.

True security exists
when the self can
meet all your needs.

Most of you think that to have security you must find something or somebody in the outer world who will give you something that will make you feel secure. No one can give you anything before you give it to yourself. If you cannot give it to yourself, then no one else can give it to you, either. This means that anything you are seeking right now to feel secure — such as money, a job, a boyfriend or girlfriend, marriage, a home — none of those will fulfill that need until you have given yourself inner security.

Some of the things people think they need to feel secure are acknowledgment and recognition, praise, love, fame, and fortune. Often love is demanded from others in a very specific way — so many phone calls a week, so many hugs, so many times the other person says, "I love you." Security needs can also include the need to feel the world is safe, to feel that you are special, to feel a part of something. Many of you look to others to give this to you, and you find constant disappointment. You can satisfy your security needs yourself — you can love yourself, believe that the world is safe, and acknowledge and recognize your accomplishments. Ultimately, only you, not other people, can fulfill these needs for yourself.

Many of you, in your search for a higher purpose, select other people and their lives as your purpose. You want to get wrapped up in their lives, draw them close to you, have them listen to your every word, cater to your slightest whim, and be swept off your feet, as they say. Your desire to entwine your life with other people's lives, to be more involved in their future than in your own, can cover up the need to fulfill your own higher purpose. When you seek to feel secure by making other people your project before you have made your own growth a priority, you will find constant disappointment in the outcome. At the very least, you will find that you cannot meet the need for self-growth by making other people's growth your life's work.

Security comes from having something in your life that is bigger than yourself, something you are reaching for, something that attracts, pulls, and calls to you. It makes the petty hurts and insignificant events small by comparison. Yet many of you seek that bigger thing in each other, rather than in your own growth.

To feel secure you need to feel you are growing, expanding, and enlarging the scope of your world.

You might think you will feel more secure by keeping things unchanged, maintaining the status quo. Yet, security only comes from taking a risk, opening up, and discovering more of who you are. Some people have discovered when they try to keep their world safe by not taking risks they end up even more scared and insecure. Facing fear always lessens it. You may have noticed when you did something new you felt braver and stronger in other areas also.

Balance is handling the amount of things you have to deal with every day in a way that is peaceful and healthy to you, and in a way that contributes to your growth and higher good. It keeps the things you are doing stimulating, helping you to wake up in the morning feeling that life is worthwhile. Decide that you will become a radiating source of stability and balance for those around you. Give yourself the things you require for joy and be willing to accept a peaceful Universe when it comes.

Achieving Balance, Stability, and Security
Playsheet

1. If you would like to have more balance, stability, and security in your life, affirm that this is your intention.

2. Sit quietly and relax your body. Take a deep breath in, and allow yourself to grow more peaceful. Ask your innermost self to assist you in experiencing feelings of balance, stability, and security more often.

3. Stay in this quiet, relaxed state and think about what you could do right now to bring more balance and stability into your daily activities, job, relationships, the pace of your life, and anything else that comes to mind.

4. Choose one or two specific actions you could take right away to feel more balanced, stable, and secure in each of the areas you thought about. Ask your innermost self to assist you in having the wisdom and courage to take these actions.

5. Make a commitment to taking these actions, then picture yourself doing so.

DAILY JOY PRACTICE

Start your day in a balanced, calm, and stable space. Make contact with your innermost self, and allow its wisdom, love, and joy to pour through you. Feel how much more centered and stable you feel with this contact.

Think of the day ahead and affirm your intention to stay balanced no matter what you are doing. Decide you will do whatever it takes to feel good physically, emotionally, and mentally. Affirm that you will take care of yourself, keep your energy stable, and maintain an open channel to your innermost self. Make up your mind that you will honor yourself today through living your life at a pace that is comfortable and nurturing to you.

Call upon your innermost self to open the way for your energy to be balanced, calm, and stable throughout the day. As you think about your day, let your innermost self show you anything you could do differently, add to, or change about your day to feel more balanced. You might ask your deepest self to alert you to any time you are not in balance, so that you can take the necessary steps to return to a stable, balanced state.

As you imagine yourself going about the day, picture yourself pausing every so often to open to your soul's energy and light, simply by thinking about doing so. Imagine doing this as you finish something, before starting the next thing, or at any other time when you want more balance, stability, security, or guidance. Picture yourself following the flow of your energy as you move from one activity or interaction to another, doing everything in a balanced, flowing, joyful, and peaceful way. Observe in your mind's eye how other people feel around you as you maintain a state of balance and stability no matter what is occurring. Your balance and stability become a gift to everyone around you.

Reflect on how you might feel at the end of the day as you maintain contact with your innermost self, which allows you to stay in a peaceful, poised, stable, balanced state all day. Note your energy level, your sense of inner peace, your clear mind, your feeling of rest and relaxation, and any other benefits that come to mind from maintaining this state.

AFFIRMATIONS

I pause often to link with my soul and
receive its energy and light.

I call in the wisdom of my innermost being
before I speak or act.

I take time to think before I act.

I take all the time I need to do a good job.

I have a positive, optimistic outlook.

I love feeling balanced.

I stay balanced and in my center at all times.

My life is balanced. I am balanced.

I stay balanced around others who are acting
in unbalanced ways.

I acknowledge all the things I am doing well.

My emotions are calm like a clear mountain lake.

I do those things that bring me aliveness.

I do those things that allow me to accomplish
my purpose with joy.

I release the need for acknowledgment, recognition,
or praise to feel good about myself.

My personal and spiritual growth is a priority in my life.

I am growing and expanding every day.

I am strong and capable.

I am creative and wise.

CHAPTER THIRTEEN

Clarity:
Living in More Light

A chieving clarity involves seeing the larger picture, a longer time frame, a bigger perspective. The larger your view, the clearer you can be. The ability of a great master to know the purpose of a soul in this lifetime brings clarity of vision and advice. How can you develop this kind of clarity in your own life?

Most of you only think about your life in terms of a time frame that involves days and weeks, rather than a period or perspective of many years, or even your entire life span. If you are willing to look at your life as a whole, you can find different levels of clarity around the present moment. You do not need to know the specific form that things will appear in, such as having a certain job title, or where you are going, such as the type of career you will have. However, the larger the picture you hold of who you are, the clearer you can be. If you were to go into the future and look back at today, you could gain a new perspective of who you are, for changing your perspective can bring clarity. Most of you have certain ways you think, certain habits and patterns. Every time you break free and find a new way of thinking, you increase clarity.

Clarity is not something that you reach and have from then on. It is an ongoing refinement of your picture. Imagine a boat trying to find a place to land near the shore. There is heavy fog, and the people in the boat cannot see anything, so they do not leave the boat nor do they take any action. As the fog lifts and they continue to look, they begin to see the fuzzy outline of the horizon and the shore. Still, they do not know what is there, so they do not take any action. Soon, as the fog dissolves, the picture becomes clear. They now know what lies ahead, and so they prepare for action.

It is the same process with clarity. At first, ideas seem vague and foggy, for that is the way essence becomes form. As the perceptual process begins, a new idea or a new way of looking at things emerges, vague in form. Often, you may only have an inner sense that something you have now is not right. This may start as an uncomfortable feeling, for the process of gaining clarity is also the process of letting go of confusion. It may be a longing, a desire, a want, or a need that will only become part of your emotional awareness after it passes through your perceptions.

Things do not usually suddenly become clear, as gaining clarity is an ongoing process. When you first feel that vague dissatisfaction, that sense that something needs to be changed, ask yourself, "How can I fine-tune this picture?" The more precise you can be about your experience, the more quickly you will gain clarity. Take any area of vague discomfort, of fogginess, and focus upon it to the exclusion of all other thoughts. Pin down precisely what the uncomfortable feeling is. If you were to focus upon that vagueness, putting words into it, trying out different thoughts about it, you would finally find a viewpoint that clicked. Once you find that viewpoint, you have clarity. Clarity comes from seeking and finding the information you need, from having the patience to seek out the light of wisdom that will assist in making the higher choice.

Clarity often involves a way of looking at things where you put them into a usable format by fitting them with and adjusting them to who you are, so you may proceed with action. Action is always preceded by a decision, and a decision is arrived at through clarity, if you are operating from your highest level.

What is the value of clarity? What will it do for you to be clear? It will save you much time; in fact, it can save years of being on a slower path of evolution. Being clear means taking the time to think out issues in your life. It is more important to think them out than to act them out. Many of you want to take action, to see results. Finding right action is quite easy if you are willing to spend the time to think, to connect with your higher, innermost self, and to receive inner guidance.

Clarity comes from a
state of mental concentration,
of focusing the thoughts,
and paying attention.

You can reach clarity by training your mind to be precise and accurate in its definition of experience. Clarity means that you are focused and living at a level of energy that others cannot interfere with. The clearer your energy is, the less affected you will be by other people, by their expectations or desires, and the clearer will be your path in life. You need clarity not just to carry out your life's purpose but in every area of your life.

Be *clear* on your intent. What do you intend to do with your life? To grow? To be loving? To be joyful? To serve, to heal? The higher your level of clarity around this, the more that clear energy will flow out into every area of your life. Your life purpose is the most important thing you can get clear about. Clarity of purpose will direct clear energy into every other area of your life. You may say, "What is life purpose, in essence?" It is the deepest desires within you, that which gives you the most joy, that which you think of and fantasize about all the time. It is that deep soul-level urge, that motivation; it is the dream that you hold within you.

How do you intend to carry out your life purpose? Even more important, do you intend to do it? Clarity of intent is the picture, the vision you are creating. When you intend to do something, you may or may not have a clear picture of the end product or the goal. Clarity of intent is a picture of where you are going or the process you want to experience in getting there. You may simply want to create a happy life or to be clear in your intent to get something done.

After clarity of intent comes clarity of motivation. What is your motivation for doing something? Whatever action you take, you want to be clear about why you are doing it. What do you see as the gain? What do you want out of it? You may realize that you were not clear before you took an action when the results are not what you expected. You may have created something you thought you wanted in your life and found it was not what you wanted. If you had been clear about what you wanted, about what you expected to gain, it would have been easier for the Universe to bring it to you in many different ways and forms.

There is also clarity of agreement. In every personal relationship, in every business relationship, and within every group, there are unspoken agreements. The more you can speak about and surface any unspoken agreements, the clearer you will be. Many disappointments and problems occur when agreements are not clear, when one person follows one set of agreements and another person follows a different set. Both can be operating from clarity, but if they are not communicating, there can be confusion and disappointment.

Careful communication brings clarity.

Clarity of communication means being precise and accurate when you speak. It means not exaggerating your experience, making bad things worse, making good things glamorous. Any tendency to exaggerate can create an imprecise communication between yourself and others. It creates unfocused, even negative experiences. Watch your words when you speak to others. Are you reflecting accurately your experience, or are you communicating to impress, dazzle, or gain sympathy? Be clear on what you want to gain when you speak to others. Are you hoping the other person will give you certain things? Are you operating from any unspoken agreements? It is important to clearly communicate what you expect if you do not want to be disappointed. Communication is one area that shapes the life you live and the forms you attract. When you speak precisely and clearly, when you know the intent of your communication, you will find your experience of others and the world improving.

Get clear on your purpose, intent, and motivation.

When you are clear on your purpose, your intent, your motivation, your agreements, when you are clear in your communications, action flows. Many of you want to start with clarity of action, and yet the true starting point is clarity of purpose. Clarity of perception lets you create the vision that matches your motivation, inner self, and core being.

Clarity in a spiritual sense is an alignment of the physical, mental, and emotional bodies with the spiritual self. You can accomplish this by linking with your soul in peaceful, calm, quiet moments. From this level, clarity flows into your mind. The mind is one of your most powerful tools when it clearly receives and interprets the guidance coming from your inner-most self. If you want clarity, ask your soul to give it to you. Your soul has the answers, as well as a connection to the flows of energy in the earth plane that will bring you abundance, love, and peace, and anything else you ask for that is for your higher good.

Think now of something about which you want clarity. Imagine that you are going upward into your soul, to the innermost part of your being. Picture your soul as fine, light energy. See your soul's light, love, and energy flowing into your mind, symbolically cleaning house, rearranging your thoughts into a more open pattern that allows you to create a future that is lighter and more joyful. Feel your soul's energy coming all the way down through your body, aligning all of your bodies — mental, emotional, and physical — with its higher energy.

If you want to know more about your life purpose, or about any personal situation, then ask. You will need to create the intention and a time to hear. Take the time to sit quietly. It may not happen the first time you try. However, if you continue to create the space for the ideas to come through, that is all that is required.

Any time you create a clear, relaxed space, calm your mind, link with your soul, and ask for information, your soul will give it to you. You are like a radio receiver that can pick up various broadcasts. Your soul is always sending you the answers and guidance you need; all you need do is tune in to the information that it is offering. The more you take time to listen within, the more you will receive. The more you spend time getting clear — quiet thinking time, linking up with the higher energies within — the more you will find yourself taking actions that are entirely different from those you might have taken. You may eliminate 80 percent or more of unnecessary actions. One half hour spent thinking and getting clear can keep you from spending years on a slower path. You can evolve rapidly on a spiritual level by spending the time to get clear, asking for what you want, and opening to receive it.

Clarity: Living in More Light

PLAYSHEET

1. Reflect on something about which you feel ambivalent or confused and would like new understanding and clarity.

2. Sit quietly and relax your body. Think of the issue for a moment, then let go of it. Get very silent and go within, allowing the peace of your innermost self to permeate your being.

3. Ask for clarity and guidance from your higher self and the higher forces of the Universe. From this peaceful, relaxed state, allow new thoughts about this issue to come into your mind, inspired new thoughts brought to you by your higher self. Ask yourself:

   - What insights am I receiving about how to act or think?
   - What beliefs do I have about the outcome? Do I need to change these beliefs to a higher view?
   - What choices do I have? (Think of at least three.)
   - What do I now *intend* to do?

DAILY JOY PRACTICE

To live in more light today, begin by asking your soul to infuse you with light and clear energy. You might imagine clear light coming down from your soul, pouring into your mind, emotions, and physical body, aligning you with your spiritual self. Your soul is bringing you clear vision so you can view your life from a higher, wiser perspective. Allow yourself to feel very clear right now as you open to this brilliant light of clear seeing, thinking, and feeling.

As you think of your day ahead, imagine that you are bringing this light of clarity into every interaction with other people, every relationship in your life, and every project you are working on. You are clear about your expectations and the agreements, both spoken and unspoken, with other people. You know what you want and you communicate it with care and precision. Picture yourself doing this.

Reflect on something you are planning to do today. Ask your soul for clarity about this area and the best way to do it. From the higher perspective of your soul, consider or question whether you need to do this at all. Is today the day to do it? Pay attention to any guidance, insights, or new information that emerges about this area.

Imagine your clear light radiating outward throughout the day, transforming all the energies about you in a positive way. Picture yourself accomplishing everything you need to do today and doing this aligned with your soul, in a clear, focused state of consciousness, listening within, and following your higher guidance. Sense how you will feel at the end of the day as you live in this higher light of clarity throughout the day.

AFFIRMATIONS

I am aware of the larger picture of whatever I focus on.

I am aware of my life as a whole from the perspective
of my entire life span.

I release old habits and patterns.
I discover new ways of thinking and being.

I open to my soul's clarity that guides me
to make the best choices.

The clarity of my innermost self guides me to right action.

I am clear. I make wise choices.

I take all the time I need to arrive at good,
clear choices and decisions.

I am clear on my intent to _____.

I am clear on my intent to know _____.

I am clear on my life purpose.
I know what I am here to do, and I am doing it.

I am clear on my motivation to have or create
_____.

I intend to carry out my life purpose.

I have clear agreements with everyone in my life.

My communication with others is clear and loving.

I align my body, emotions,
and mind with my spiritual being.

My soul always responds when I ask it for more clarity.
I am clear.

I create quiet time to receive the guidance and
clarity I need from my soul.

I ask the Universe for what I want,
and I am open to receive it.

I make good decisions and choices.

I take time to be quiet every day and listen within.

I hold every situation up to the clear light of my soul,
knowing that a higher solution always exists.

CHAPTER FOURTEEN

Freedom Is Your Birthright

Freedom is an inner feeling. It is the ability to choose what you want. It is the knowledge that *you* are the captain of the ship. Freedom is knowing that you own your own life, that you are the one in charge. Freedom is essential for joy, for anywhere you feel trapped or that someone has taken away your rights, you cannot experience joy.

Freedom is important if you are to bring the light of your soul into your consciousness. You live on a planet of free will, where you learn about action and reaction, cause and effect. Earth reality is based on choice. No matter what situation you are experiencing in your life, whether you *think* you have freedom or not, you have made a choice to be in that situation, whether or not you were aware of making that choice.

You learn by trial and error. Do not make yourself or others wrong for the choices being made, for everyone is always growing through the outcomes and results of their actions. In this earth school of free will you call life there are many lessons and challenges of freedom.

*The only limits to freedom
are those you place upon yourself.*

How do you lose your sense of joyous freedom, your birthright of choice? As a small child, you have many demands and expectations placed on you, yet a child has more freedom than it might appear. A child is free to respond in new ways, to learn and to grow without preconceived ideas. A child is free to examine things afresh, to take each experience for what it is and not categorize or analyze it based on past experiences. A child is free, particularly in the earlier years of life, to form opinions based not on past ideas but on natural reactions.

As a child grows, some feelings of freedom become lost in the process of developing the mind. The mind begins to look for patterns; it begins to see associations, connecting things that it would do better to understand as independent events. When something happens, the mind looks at all other things of a similar nature, often exaggerating the negative by comparing the current situation to memories of the past.

As a child, you make strong decisions. A man who often felt afraid to stand by his creative work discovered that when he was a young child someone had ridiculed a picture he had painted. He became afraid to show people his creative work. He began to hide his drawings, and eventually he felt bad about every creative effort. He became afraid to assert his power. He identified new experiences with the old one, and in this way he froze the degree of choice available in new but similar circumstances. This led to a loss of freedom — he was no longer free to choose his response to his own power and creativity.

Children make constant and ongoing decisions about the nature of reality. One woman found it difficult to speak out about things she really believed in. She discovered that as a small child, when making a cake, her mother had sharply rebuked her for a comment she made. She made a decision at that moment — that to be lovable, she needed to keep her opinions to herself. In future situations she operated on that premise. It took away her freedom to respond spontaneously and to see each situation as a new experience. She became afraid to speak up, and she found herself intimidated when it came to voicing an opinion that someone might challenge.

Freedom is your birthright. It belongs to everyone. Now you may say, I am not free in this or that area of my life. I am not free to quit my job, travel the world, or do what I want. You are free — to the degree you believe yourself to be free.

To create more freedom in your life,
do not look at the areas in
which you do not have freedom;
look instead at the areas
where you have created freedom.

Perhaps you have the freedom to stay out late if you want, or the freedom to buy a special food you want at the grocery store. To have more freedom, look at what freedom you already claim as your right. You put yourself in the role of a victim when you feel sorry for yourself for lacking freedom. Whenever you experience yourself in that role, you are not powerful. Look instead at the areas in which you have chosen not to be the victim of another person or a circumstance. All of you have created freedom in many areas of your life. You can see that you have given yourself many freedoms, freedoms you value greatly and would allow no one to take away.

How about those areas in your life where people are demanding more from you than you want to give? They may want more time, energy, love, or attention. They may demand it in such a way that you feel a loss of freedom. If this is occurring in your life, try asking yourself if a part of you wants more time and more attention from another part of you than you are willing to give. Anything that you feel another person is taking away from you is symbolic of something you are taking from yourself. If you feel people want more attention than you can give them, or put demands on you that you cannot and do not choose to meet, ask, "Is a part of me putting demands that cannot be met on another part of myself?"

Other people act as mirrors to show you something about what you are doing to yourself. In this case, you can ask, "Am I in some way taking something away from myself, not paying enough attention to my own needs?" You can begin by looking at what those needs are and deciding you will pay attention to them. In one case, a man felt his girlfriend was demanding far too much from him in the way of time and space. He enjoyed his many hours spent working alone, and her need for companionship was far greater than his was. As he began to examine the demands she put on him for more attention, he realized that in all of his long hours of work he was not paying attention to himself and his own greater needs. He discovered he was not paying attention to his innermost self, which wanted sleep and rest and more attention. He was instead working long, hard hours, ignoring his physical needs and the needs of other parts of himself.

The woman who felt this man was not giving her the attention and the time she wanted began to look at this as an inner message. She felt they did not play or spend quality time together. On deeper reflection, she realized that she was not giving herself quality time, that she was rushing around all day, responding to the needs of others, and that she was not allowing herself to play and have fun. Everything she blamed her partner for withholding from her was something she was not giving herself.

Freedom is something you create for yourself. Freedom is not given to you, and it cannot be taken away. You can choose to give it away, and you can choose not to claim it, but others cannot take it. Only you can give it away. There are many areas of freedom in your life you know *nobody* would be able to take away from you. Perhaps you have a favorite place to eat and you feel free to eat there. You know deep inside that no one would be able to stop you. Perhaps you have the freedom to watch a favorite show on TV, or listen to music you love, and you know no one will stop you. You may notice in these situations that nobody does try to stop you.

> *When you put out a definite and clear message to the Universe, you rarely have to fight for what you want.*

Have you ever rehearsed something in advance, gotten very clear about what you wanted, and then discovered you did not even need to ask for it because once you got clear, the other person did not even challenge you? Struggling to get what you want most often happens when you are not certain you deserve to have it.

Many of you who work feel that you are not free, that in some way or another between the hours of nine and five you have given up your freedom. Freedom is an attitude. To experience freedom in this situation, it may be necessary to look at the larger picture. Why are you in this job? If it is for the money, remember that you freely chose this job to make money and that you are free at any time to find another way to make money.

You can create a sense of freedom from moment to moment by realizing you are free to respond, act, and feel any way you choose. You are free to speak and take action within the framework of your job. You can always find a level of freedom in everything you do. Look at where you are free. Focus on that freedom, and it will increase in your life.

The greatest barrier to freedom lies in the way you think of the world. Lack of freedom does not come from other people, but from your own thinking processes. Many of you take away your freedom by not allowing yourselves a choice of how to react to a given situation. For instance, say your friend always criticizes you, and you always respond with hurt or anger. You can gain freedom by finding new ways to react.

Perhaps you can say, "Oh, this friend of mine simply does not know a better way to act." Or, "Perhaps this friend of mine is very critical of himself or herself, and is only criticizing me because it is the way that my friend talks to himself or herself." You can choose to come from compassion and not take the criticism personally. You can choose to remain centered and balanced even when others around you are not. This is the ultimate freedom, the freedom to choose how you will respond and be, the freedom to act in a way that elevates your energy.

Most people respond in habitual ways, rather than examining their responses. Realize that you can choose how you react and respond to everything in the Universe. When some people have deadlines, they look over what they need to do, and then take the steps needed to complete their project peacefully, even with time to spare. Others may feel panicked and start rushing through it to get the project done. Other people respond by procrastinating and finishing at the last moment. Still others respond with depression, feeling that the task is overwhelming, with their inner voice telling them they can never do it, so they only do a halfhearted job. You are free to choose — do you want to react to something in a way that makes you feel unhappy or bad about yourself, or do you want to react in a way that promotes your self-worth and self-esteem?

Other people respond to you in whatever way their programs and beliefs dictate. Power comes in knowing that you have a choice. You do not need to change other people; you can change your reaction to them. When you choose to feel good you are not dependent on other people acting in certain ways to make you feel good. Before you can attract people who will support, appreciate, and acknowledge you, you must choose to do that for yourself.

The degree to which you support and acknowledge yourself will be the degree to which you receive support.

Each time you choose to feel good about yourself, even when someone is criticizing you, putting you down, or acting in a way that you used to respond to with pain, you are choosing joy. Each time you do so you create freedom in your life. You are free from needing other people to act in certain ways for you to be happy. You are free from your own expectations.

Frequently a feeling of pain comes from getting caught in details rather than seeing the larger picture. For instance, a woman became very disappointed in her boyfriend when he did not bring her flowers. She had the picture in her mind that receiving flowers from men meant that they loved her. Every time she thought about him not bringing flowers, she felt pain. She was not free to choose joy because of her own internal pictures. When she began to look at the truth and the larger picture, she realized that this man loved her deeply, was very committed to her, and did not view giving flowers as a statement of love. As she looked at all the good things that existed between them, she realized she was getting caught in her own expectations; she was choosing pain out of habit.

To have freedom
be willing to give freedom.

You cannot own another person, nor can you have a relationship of equality when you are taking freedom away from someone else. All people have the right to do what is enlivening and growth-oriented for them. Many people have to leave relationships because they are not given the freedom they need to grow. Some feel threatened by the need for freedom in their partner or mate. They may interpret a request for freedom as rejection, thinking the other person is pulling away from them, rather than as the other's attempt to seek out his or her own higher self.

Ironically, the more freedom you give people, the more they will want to be with you. Do you demand things of others that you would not want them to demand of you? Do you expect them to report in to you, live up to your pictures, and be there whenever you want? Whatever degree of freedom you take from others is the degree of freedom you take from yourself.

Imagine a prisoner sitting in a cell with a guard who must guard him twenty-four hours a day. The question is, who is really the prisoner? If you feel that you must watch over or guard others all the time, that you cannot trust them or give them freedom, you are just as trapped as they are. Many of you lose your freedom because you are so closely guarding those things that you do not want taken away from you. You may guard your mate, your possessions, your children, or your family in such a way that you are spending more time protecting them than seeking your own growth.

If you experience jealousy, it may be based on a fear that others are giving something to someone else that they are not giving to you. If you look and examine the issue, it is usually something you are not giving yourself. If you are jealous of your mate giving attention to another person, and you want to curtail his or her freedom so that he or she cannot do so, think again. It may be that you are not giving yourself, your life, or your higher self the necessary attention for your own well-being and spiritual growth.

Jealousy takes away the freedom of both the one who is jealous and the one who is possessed. If you give yourself what you need — be it attention, love, or something else — then you will not experience jealousy. You will find that you can get satisfaction from many sources, not just from the one you love. Jealousy implies scarcity, that there is not enough. Freedom implies abundance, that there is enough.

Determine now that
you will give freedom
to everyone close to you.

Let others make their own mistakes and discover their own joys. I can guarantee that anytime you give freedom to others, they will turn to you with greater love and respect. It takes a centered, balanced, and secure person to give others their freedom. It is a great gift to them and to yourself, for when one no longer needs to guard the prisoner, the jailer is also free.

You are free when you can choose how you want to respond. If you can choose to react with joy and pleasure, if you can choose to react by seeing the positive, making yourself right rather than wrong, then you have gained the ultimate freedom, the freedom to be and act in a way that reflects your deeper truth.

Freedom Is Your Birthright
PLAYSHEET

1. Remember at least three areas in which you allow yourself freedom.

2. Are there any areas in your life where you do *not* feel free? For example: I am not free to go back to school or quit my job.

3. Can you imagine it is possible to have freedom in those areas of your life? If it is possible, start picturing yourself having freedom in these areas. Give yourself permission to make the needed changes in these areas. It may take a while for freedom to appear in your daily life, but freedom starts with the thought of it. Turn every statement above into a positive affirmation in those areas you feel freedom is possible. For example: I am now free to go back to school.

DAILY JOY PRACTICE

Determine that today you will experience more freedom in every area of your life. Connect with your soul and give it permission to assist you in releasing anything that stands in the way of your freedom. Imagine breathing in the quality of freedom that releases obstacles, blockages, and limitations, opening the way to having more freedom in your life.

As you think of the day ahead, realize how free you really are, even though you may not think you are free in certain areas. Throughout the day acknowledge and affirm your freedom, no matter what you are doing. Recognize that you are free to feel, respond, and think however you choose. Say to yourself with feeling, "I am free. I am the captain of my ship. I am in charge of my life!"

If you are doing something you do not want to do and do not feel free to stop doing it, remind yourself why you chose to do this in the first place. If it is no longer appropriate to continue this activity or if you no longer want to do it, draw in the energy of freedom from your soul. Ask it to assist you in letting go of this activity. Ask for assistance to find and create wonderful new opportunities.

Throughout the day, every time you have a choice or decision to make, pause for a moment, draw in the energy of freedom, and ask your innermost self to release any limitations. Ask for guidance to create a more expansive, higher future. Realize how easily you can release any limits you have placed on yourself simply by asking for help from your innermost self. Give yourself the greatest freedom of all — the freedom to receive and act upon the inner guidance that comes from your innermost self. Recognize and acknowledge that you are free, because you are!

AFFIRMATIONS

I am free to listen to and follow my inner guidance.

I am the captain of my ship. I am in charge of my life!

I release any limits to my freedom I have placed on myself.

I acknowledge all the ways I am free.

I am free to act, feel, and respond in whatever way I choose.

I am free from the past.
My future is an open book I am creating anew every day.

I am free from attachments.

I stay free by not taking personally what others say or do. I
know that their actions and words are a reflection
of who they are, not who I am.

I change my relationships by changing myself.

I give others the freedom to be who they are.

I give others the freedom to live their lives as they see fit.

I act in ways that reflect my deepest truth.

I am free. My life is my own.

Everything I do I *choose* to do.

I release all limitations. I live in a limitless world.

CHAPTER FIFTEEN

Embracing the New

Being open to accept new things, ideas, and people into your life creates an ever-expanding capacity for joy. There is a mass thoughtform that the future might be worse than the present. This creates the need to hang on to what you have, freeze things as they are, and keep them from changing. Doing this can lead to much pain.

Embracing the new means being open to having more in your life. Many of you think that what you have created up until now is the best you can do. You make something and think that the first try is your best. However, on the second and third tries you may do even better. As you create things in your life, you become better and more skilled. That is the process of life. A child who first begins walking is wobbly and unsteady. As the child practices, he or she becomes strong and steady in his or her stride. It is the same with everything you do, for life is like a spiral in which you circle around again and again, often to the same issues, but each time from a higher perspective.

Opening to new things means trusting and having faith in yourself and others. It means believing that the future holds joy and promise. It means believing in your growth and direction. The heart is the center of faith, trust, and belief. Opening to the new means opening your heart. Be willing to step outside of your normal limits and viewpoints and see the world in different ways. Trust that the world is safe and know that you are the director and the producer of what occurs in your life.

Opening to the new takes a willingness to view the old not with hate, anger, or disgust, but with compassion. Many of you leave a relationship in anger, or you buy a new car when you are mad at your old one. That is one way to leave the old and embrace the new. As you follow the path of joy you can learn to open to new things while you are in a state of acceptance and peace with the old.

When things are not going well in your life, sometimes you gather the motivation and energy to change them by becoming angry or choosing pain. It need not be difficult to leave the old and embrace the new. If you start thinking of what you want, how you would like your life to be, you begin easily and automatically to draw the new to yourself. If you want something and it can only come when another person changes or acts differently, then you do not have power or control over that. You only have power or control over your own emotions and reactions.

If you want something new,
be open to having it come
from anywhere, any place, any person.

Be open to surprises and new things. Keep your heart open. Some of you experience a feeling of vulnerability or fear when you think of bringing new people or new things into your lives. What you call tension or anxiety before an event can be viewed instead as focusing your energy to prepare you for something new. This change in your vibration prepares you for something that is finer and higher in your life. You may feel that you must first conquer fear and anxiety before you step out and accomplish something. Everyone has that inner feeling of tension to some degree before attempting new things; it is a period of gathering energy to make the shift into a higher vibration.

Everything that happens to you assists you in bringing yourself to a higher level of evolution. Even those things you call negative or bad occur to show you new ways of responding so that you may be more balanced, peaceful, and joyful in the future. If it looks like the same problem or situation is occurring over and over, be aware that every single time it happens in a new way. Embrace what is new about that pattern or situation and look at how you have succeeded in bringing it to a higher level. Perhaps you are more aware of it than before or able to understand it better. You may be less emotionally involved and more able to observe the pattern. Every day brings with it new circumstances, challenges, and activities that allow you the opportunity to grow.

An attitude of openness and receptivity will draw to you many good things. Let go of the fear that the future may mean having less than you have now or may take something away from you. Open up to the idea that you will be wiser, stronger, and more powerful tomorrow and that whatever you create will be even better than what you already have. Be open to new concepts and words. They are often the way the Universe brings you the signs and guideposts of your next step.

You can experience opening to the new in many ways. Many of you have a need for aliveness, excitement, and adventure. Often you blame your partner because life seems dull and routine, or you blame your job for its monotony. You can create that sense of aliveness in everything you do, and you can do it in simple ways. Change your morning routine, get up earlier, go to bed later, or change what you do when you get home from work. Even minor changes can stimulate a sense of aliveness.

Every time you
embrace something new,
you bring into yourself
a sense of aliveness.

Your heart expands, and you literally begin revitalizing yourself and rejuvenating your body, as you embrace new things. Life always seeks growth, expansion, and evolution. As you experience the new, you can see more of who you are. You do not need to make the old ways wrong; rather, create newness in the old. Only when you do not see the new in the old does growth cease and relationships become dull.

You may have seen people who have been together for many years and who act vibrant and young and in love. If you examine the relationship, you will discover that they are doing new things, creating new projects, and bringing a sense of aliveness into their personal lives. They are probably conquering new territory, opening to adventure, and feeling alive individually, in whatever way is appropriate for them. People who have been together for a long time and seem irritated or bored with each other often take each other for granted. They may go to bed at the same time every night, awake and go to the same job, and do the same things on the weekend. All of that leads to a sense of contraction around the heart and a sense of boredom and deadness inside, which is then reflected in the relationship.

Opening to the new is a way of feeling more youthful, of expanding your childlike sense of wonder and awe. As they grow older, many people constrict their boundaries; they often seek what is comfortable, familiar, and safe. Their world becomes increasingly narrow and limited. Life becomes a matter of focusing on the petty rather than on the great. You have seen those people whose concerns are so minor you do not take them seriously, or people who are so focused on what is bad and wrong with the world they become fearful of the new and no longer experience joy. They have ceased to expand into the greater picture of their lives and have stopped embracing all the potential that lies within them.

There is a new you every day.

Every morning when you wake up you are literally being born anew and afresh. Every day there are new things on your mind, people to meet, things to do. As you wake up and start your day, you need not think of the past and remember mistakes; instead, focus upon the future and what you will create.

Try out new routines each day. When you do new things you are conscious and aware of the present moment. You are paying attention, fully alert. Doing new things is invigorating to the physical body. Try bringing this same alertness to whatever you normally do to experience familiar activities in new ways.

You do many things without having to consciously think about them. Your breathing and many of your bodily functions are automatically controlled. As a child your nervous system develops in such a way that it learns to select information, for if too much information is coming in, there is a lack of focus. In the development of your being, there is a learned balance between focusing upon those things that need to be paid attention to and not being sidetracked by meaningless, trivial, and constant irrelevant data. As a child you developed selective awareness, tuning out many things in your Universe so that you could tune in to others.

The ability to do many things routinely and habitually without much thought gives you more time and energy to focus on new things that do require thought and attention. However, many of you react automatically to those things that you should examine. Some of the things you do routinely without questioning may be creating discomfort and a lack of well-being.

Attempting new things can prompt you to reexamine all of the habitual and routine things you take for granted. Some people choose jobs that involve danger or tension so they can experience the awareness and attention required to stay alive. These jobs require them to live in the present moment, focused and fully alert, such as race car drivers and mountain climbers. A feeling of aliveness comes when you are not operating on automatic but are fully conscious and aware of every action. You do not have to engage in dangerous jobs to feel alive. As you embrace the new, you begin to bring into consciousness those things that may have been routine. You can then experience present-time awareness and live in the moment.

*Power comes from
living in the present moment,
where you can take
action and create the future.*

As you embrace the new, remember things are always going to get better. The Universe does not take anything away unless something better is coming. Every down cycle is followed by a great leap forward. It is easy to embrace the new. Play like a child. You have seen how children embrace everything as a new experience. It can be easy to open up and embrace the new if you picture it as easy. Keep a picture in your mind that the future is positive and that it will be better than anything you have ever known. As you grow and evolve, what you create will be even more joyous than what you have now.

Embracing the New
PLAYSHEET

1. Think of at least three new things, skills, or experiences you brought into your life last year. As you list them, think of how you felt as you learned them or brought them into your life.

2. From today's perspective, how did doing these new things, learning these new skills, or having these new experiences contribute to your life? What new opportunities came about from your embracing the new in these areas?

3. Now, think about at least three new experiences or skills that you would like to bring into your life next year. Set your intention to do these things; join with your innermost being, your soul and higher self; open to its light and energy; and affirm that you *will* bring these new experiences, opportunities, and skills into your life.

DAILY JOY PRACTICE

Open to the joy of what lies ahead today, tomorrow, or even during the next hour. Affirm that you are ready to embrace the new, to become aware of new ways to feel more alive, revitalized, and present in every moment. Release any predetermined pictures of what your day might be like and experience the day fresh, allowing things to be different from what you might have expected or planned. Decide to be more spontaneous and open to all possibilities as they unfold.

Connect with your innermost self and ask for its assistance in embracing new ways of feeling, being, speaking, and acting today. Be alert to new, creative thoughts, activities, and experiences. Explore how you can do something you normally do in a fresh, innovative way. If you realize you are doing something out of habit, stop, connect with your innermost self, and ask to be shown a new way to act. Allow into your mind right now a few pictures and thoughts about how you can experience and embrace the new you today.

Feel the joy in embracing the new today. Note how each day is a fresh start, a new chapter in your life. Each day you are a new you, stronger and more loving, with greater wisdom and more understanding. Sense the increased aliveness that comes just by thinking about bringing fresh energy into your life and living in new ways. You are expanding into a higher future of infinite possibilities.

AFFIRMATIONS

I expand my capacity for joy by embracing the new.

I believe in myself.

I am the director and producer of my life.

I peacefully and lovingly release situations and
relationships that are not for my higher good.

Everything in my life is bringing me
to a higher level of evolution.

I view every situation as an opportunity to grow stronger
and more joyful.

I am open and receptive to experiencing new situations,
people, and activities.

I experience more aliveness as I embrace the new.

I am growing, expanding, and evolving.

Everything I do energizes me. I am glad to be alive!

I bring my full attention to whatever I am doing or saying.

I am conscious and aware of the present moment.

I attract fresh, positive experiences.

I embrace the new, knowing that my life is
always getting better.

My future holds joy and promise.

I am receptive to the infinite, expansive, and
wonderful possibilities that exist for me.

I have many new thoughts, insights, and experiences.

I am growing and expanding in ways that are joyful
and balanced.

I love growth. I am on a path of enlightenment.

CHAPTER SIXTEEN

Taking a Quantum Leap

N ew ideas and forward movements do not always come
in the form the mind expects. In picturing the highest
good for yourself it is important that you use your mind to go
upward. First let your mind come up with the initial images of
what you want. As the mind creates pictures, those images go
upward and inward to the light of the soul, to your innermost
being. The soul then gives the mind new ideas and visions. It
may seem at times that you think of what you want, and by the
time you get it, it is different from what you originally asked
for. This is because the mind, when requesting something,
automatically activates the resources of the greater self. When
the request comes back, it comes back in its higher form.

You may wonder why some of the things you ask for take
a long time to come. Quantum leaps involve time and your
ability to manifest. Quantum leaps happen when you make
large, life-affirming changes, going from one way of being to

another. They often involve a major change in your perspective, a letting go of some major belief, or an opening to a higher understanding that changes your life. Taking a quantum leap may involve changing your desires or letting go of a comfortable, secure existence and taking a risk. It may mean committing to bringing something better into your life, to believing in yourself — inner transformations that can lead to many changes in your daily life as well.

If you go back and look at what you have asked for in the past, you will see that many of the things you did not get, you no longer want, and the things that were for your higher good, you have. Some things that you may be preparing to have may come later, or come in a different way or form than you expected.

Your soul shows you how to get things, not through the mind, but through your feelings, inner messages, and emotions. After you get clear on what you want to create, listen to your spontaneous and creative urges. They may seem to have no relationship to the goal you want to reach. It may seem as if, for instance, you put out for great financial success, and all of a sudden you want to take the summer off and study something else, or you lose your job.

As you trust your inner urges and study something else, you may find new ideas emerging that eventually bring you the wealth you wanted. As you search for a new job, you may find an even better job than the one you had. Or, you may discover that you now have more time to explore who you are and what you truly want out of life, or you have the time to develop a hobby or learn new skills. You may decide to start your own business. Your soul is always telling you the highest, most expansive, and best way to go, but you will need to take the leap of faith and trust and act upon your inner guidance.

*If you are going for
a major change in your life,
you will want to change
those beliefs that kept you
from having it in the past.*

If you are very clear in your intent to get from one place to another — for instance, from one level of financial prosperity to another, or from one level of creative success to another — then you must undergo changes in yourself. Because, if you have already reached the understanding, wisdom, and awareness that are necessary to create these things, you would not need to do anything. You would already have what you want. A woman said, "I want to be a millionaire. Today I cannot pay my rent, but I want to be a millionaire, and I would like to have it as quickly as possible." If she *believed* she could have it, she would have already accomplished it by that point.

When you put a request for a quantum leap out to the Universe, the request goes upward from your mind to your spirit, the innermost part of your being. Your spirit then begins broadcasting signals back to your mind, telling you how to create the changes you want. Now, you must pay attention to those signals. Changes will need to happen on many levels for you to achieve this new step.

For instance, in our example of greater financial prosperity, the woman might need to learn many of the principles of creating money. Therefore, her soul may direct her to read many books or may send someone to her who can teach and instruct her, if she is not willing to let go of her past images of lack of money. It may be that her heart is not yet open enough to believe that she can receive and deserve that kind of money. There will be many lessons sent to her to help open her heart. In fact, her level of trust may be so undeveloped that her ability to make money cannot happen until she develops more faith and trust in herself.

Whatever you ask for, you may have to let go of something to get it. If you have asked for money, you may have to let go of your images of the lack of it, of all of the ways you live that reflect those images, and of the ways you spend and save. Your soul will give you many challenges and growth opportunities to help you let go of those images of lack. The money may come at first in small amounts so that you can demonstrate your willingness to spend on those things that create prosperity. Eventually, as you change your energy, as you rewrite your programs, decisions, and beliefs, ideas will begin flowing — specific, concrete ideas about how to create the money and abundance you seek. It may be a year or two, or even more, before you clear up your programs around lack of abundance enough for the specific ideas to come in. At that point, you will be better able to create many ways to attract wealth and refine those ideas until they become a fact in your life.

Some people stop trying when something does not come immediately because their minds cannot see the connection between the lessons that are occurring and their request for a major change. Their minds may even interpret some of the events as taking them in the wrong direction. Although they are asking for something over and over, the opposite may seem to be occurring. However, if people look at how much they are growing by experiencing events that appear to be the opposite of what they want, they will see that in fact these events are working on their energy and opening them in certain ways to have what they are asking for.

For instance, one man asked for an increase of 100 percent in his monthly salary. Shortly thereafter, his boss reduced his salary due to business problems. It looked like he was getting the opposite of what he asked for. However, he began to think about starting his own business in a related field, something he had wanted to do for years. The cut in pay became a motivation to move forward and start his own business. He did indeed make the income he asked for, several years later, in his own business.

As you can see, change is much more involved than simply asking for something and having it come to you. You may need to go inward, expand your faith and trust, and open your heart. You may need to trust your inner guidance and impulses in order to move from your present level of abundance to a greater one. You may also need to let go of many old images about who you are. You will have many growth opportunities offered to you to change those mental images. At the soul level, it is always a joy to grow, and the soul is always concerned that you are growing. Whether you are growing through pain or joy, growth is the end goal, the growth that is required for you to have what you have decided you want. The soul lets your mind operate with a great deal of free will in choosing which goals you will bring about or what quantum leaps you want. The higher you aim with your mind, the more you will experience the spiritual growth your soul is offering you.

Your soul often speaks to you through your emotions by giving you a feeling or an urge to do something that will lead to accomplishing your goals or draw to you something you have been wanting. When you experience strong feelings and urges to do something, it is important to act upon them. Your mind may make up reasons why you should not follow an urge, for your mind follows the familiar programs it knows.

Your innermost urges come from your soul, which has a much broader picture of your higher good and knows ways to bring it to you that your mind cannot even conceive of. Your heart and feelings often lead you in directions your mind cannot anticipate.

Make a decision, as you take a quantum leap, to follow your inner guidance, the inner urges of your feelings, your heart, and your soul. Let your mind have the role of setting a goal or clear intention, and make the decision to accomplish it. Then your soul can go out in all directions and make you magnetic to the coincidences, people, and events that create what you want. This happens beyond the level of the mind; you need to follow your inner urgings, higher guidance, and heart to join this flow.

*You can choose
how quickly
you wish it to happen.*

To shorten the time between asking for what you want and receiving it, be clear on your goals. Some of you are so nonspecific that your mind wanders around, never making clear requests to your soul, and so your soul spends much time guiding your mind to get clear about what you want. The more accurately and precisely you can state what you want in any area of your life, the more rapidly you will have it. You may not get it in the precise form you asked for, but your soul will create for you the essence of what you want. It will bring it to you in the best form, in the right timing, and in a way that it will contribute positively to your life.

In being precise, you are formulating essence. Essence is the growth that you are going for in any quantum leap, and I would suggest that you take anything you have requested and ask, "What is the essence of it?" If you look at what you have already tried to create, you will see that you have always gotten the essence of everything you asked for. For instance, if you wished for a loving relationship, you may have wanted simply to feel loved. Your soul may give you love in many ways, perhaps through a close friend, child, or pet, perhaps through a job promotion, or in any of the ways you accept love. If you want to create a more fit body, the essence of what you want may be more self-love. If you are willing to go for essence in your quantum leaps, you will be able to accomplish them far more rapidly.

If you are tempted to go back into the past and say, "Well, I wanted this, but I did not get it," look at the core, at the essence, of what you requested. I would say you have gotten it in many ways. The soul is quite creative in interpreting your request. The soul has to be creative, for the mind is fairly narrow in its ability to ask. The soul takes any request for growth and expands it in every direction it can.

Emotional changes are often required for a quantum leap.

When your emotions are heavy and sad or negative, the aura around your body is dense. It is like driving with a dirty windshield. You cannot see clearly or far. The light of your soul does not come through brightly. Your soul will guide you to look at those areas in your life that are creating emotional

disturbance and to stop reacting to them. Find ways to calm
your emotions, for calm emotions speed up the time it takes to
reach your goals. When you are calm and peaceful, your soul
comes through your emotions to give you that inner guidance.
The soul gives guidance through the emotional body, in urges,
insights, and those feelings that take you into new arenas.

Taking a quantum leap does not mean searching for relief
from worry or disappointment, but creating delight and joy.
Look back at those times in which you did something great
and you will see the level of motivation and desire that led
you to create it. Often you say, "I *should* do this, or create this
or that, to make me happy." If doing those things only brings
you a sense of relief, your goals will probably remain a *should*
and not become an accomplished fact. To take a quantum
leap, you need great motivation, desire, and real inner drive to
create your goals. To succeed, your goal must be more than a
nice thing to do or something that simply feels good. It needs
to be something that you can get behind at all levels, that your
emotions can feel excited about, something that you truly
want to do, intend to do, and will commit to carrying out.

Disliking poverty, for instance, is not enough to get you
out of it. You need to truly desire and love to make money if
you want more of it. You cannot get what you want by hating
your lack of it. So ask, when you look at the quantum leap you
want to make, what *is* your motivation? If you see that there
is no motivation other than to relieve bad feelings about who
you are, ask, "What can I create as a motivation?" Those things
you create and go toward are things you feel highly charged
about, that bring you great joy and delight. You can always
find the money for something you want to do. You can always
find the time to do something that excites you. It is the same
for taking a quantum leap. If you have an area in which you

think you *should* make a big change, but you have not done it yet, ask if you really intend to do it. You know the difference.

If you are working toward quantum leaps that have not yet occurred, be aware that everything you are doing right now in your life is getting you closer. Go inward for a moment and ask, "What quantum leap am I in the process of taking? And how could something that happened in the last week or even today be preparing me to have it?"

*The mind works better if
it has fixed reference points
to mark its progress along the way.*

In some ways the mind is like a child. Children do not want to think of high school when they are two years old. They want to think of food or their friends. The mind is the same way. Create something that is delightful today or tomorrow — one small action that will bring you closer to your goal. The mind likes to have markers and feel a sense of accomplishment. What would be delightful for you to create today or tomorrow that would bring you one step closer to your higher goal? At the same time, ask yourself, "Is there any inner urging that I have right now about something I want to do that I have been putting off?" Is there something you have been thinking might take too much time or might be off course?

In these ways you can begin working with your emotions and your mind to bring a quantum leap even closer. If each day you wake up and say, "What is my inner urging, my purpose today?" and ask, "What can I create so that my mind can see I am taking action to get closer to my goal?" there will be much greater progress in your leap forward. The mind likes the sense that it has accomplished things. The emotions are also much happier when they can see progress. Be aware that the actual steps you take may not turn out to be the necessary ones. They can still be quite satisfying and bring a sense of forward movement. The mind is unable at times to connect what is going on — the phone calls, the particular problems and opportunities that come up — with forward movement.

Often you have a great picture or vision, but each little piece of the puzzle is happening in the present time and may not seem to fit the whole. Even a comment a friend makes to you, a phone call, or something you read can very much be part of your forward movement. The mind, not knowing all of the areas that you are opening to or all the beliefs that you are changing, often cannot see the pattern and forward movement. It may not think you are growing or reaching your goals. If it becomes impatient or disbelieving, it can cloud your emotions and make taking a quantum leap more difficult. If you can give your mind the satisfaction of having accomplished an action, it can also help your emotions.

Ask yourself what step you would like to take toward your goal. Ask yourself if there are any inner urges you have been getting for something you could do in the next month. It need not even seem related to your goal.

Make the decision that you will do it.

Taking a Quantum Leap
PLAYSHEET

1. What quantum leap would you like in your life?

2. Is there anything you would have to let go of to have it, such as a belief, attitude, thing, or person?

3. What is the essence of this goal? Is there any other form that will give you the essence of what you want?

4. What is your motivation to accomplish this quantum leap?

5. Often, inner urges or whispers in your mind are connected to your quantum leap, even though they may not appear to be related. Ponder on any inner urges you have been having.

6. What specific step, no matter how simple, can you take in the next week toward your goal?

DAILY JOY PRACTICE

You have the ability to accelerate your spiritual growth and make great forward progress in any area of your life, and you can do so peacefully and joyfully. You can create whatever you need that is for your highest good and bring it into your life in its best and highest form. A daily practice for taking a quantum leap is to strengthen your belief in yourself and to let go of limiting beliefs that are holding you back.

Call upon your innermost self right now to assist you in having thoughts that show you why you *can* have what you want. These are thoughts that strengthen your belief in yourself and in your ability to manifest. Know that your true, innermost self always responds when you ask for its assistance.

Today you will build yourself up in every way you can imagine. You will make yourself right rather than wrong. You will reframe the negative into the positive. You will believe in yourself and trust your inner guidance. You will acknowledge that you have the motivation and inner drive necessary to take a quantum leap. You will recognize how everything you are doing is bringing you closer to your goals in some way.

Today, affirm that you will not allow doubts, concerns, or negative pictures into your mind. You will remember your past successes and trust that everything happens for your higher good. This day is a celebration of you and your ability to take a quantum leap!

AFFIRMATIONS

I know what steps to take to bring me closer to my goals,
and I take them.

My soul is guiding me in all that I do.

I trust and act upon my inner guidance.

I grow through joy.

I ask for what I want. I am open to receiving it in whatever
way or form it appears that is for my higher good.

I no longer allow doubts, concerns,
or negative pictures into my mind.

I release limiting beliefs and open to new,
empowering beliefs.

Everything I do brings me closer to my goals.

I know that everything happens for my higher good.

I trust the Universe. I know the world is safe and
working for me.

I accept abundance, and it is coming to me now.

I have the power to create whatever I want.

I clearly state what I want.

I have the motivation and inner drive necessary
to take a quantum leap.

I believe in myself.

I am a successful person. I acknowledge all my successes.

I know the essence of what I want, and I intend to get it.

I create delight and joy in my life.

CHAPTER SEVENTEEN

Living in Higher Purpose

Higher purpose is a stream of energy you join when you create something that serves humankind or your own spiritual evolution. Without higher purpose you are a wanderer, roaming around, taking various paths with many potential wrong turns, which leads to wasted or lost time. With higher purpose, you can choose every moment, knowing what to do with each hour, each day, and each week. Living in higher purpose allows you to grow and evolve rapidly in this lifetime.

Everyone on earth has a higher purpose. You came to earth to be a part of a system of energy that deals with emotions, personality, and thoughts, that involves seeing what is inside of you reflected back to you in the outside world.

There are other universes in which forms come and go more quickly; almost the minute they are thought of, they appear and disappear. Things move more slowly on the earth plane. Time is literally slowed down so you can focus on certain things. You segmented yourself into a certain time frame called *birth to death*, and you are working on specific energies. I am speaking of the larger framework of the Universe, for compared to other dimensions and realms, the earth plane is very slow. The wave of its note is very long so that you can experience matter. From that perspective, you want to evolve upward to the highest frequency of this note, so you may go on to other places where the rules change. There are places where you are more a pure energy being, unbound by the concrete world of time, space, and matter.

Here on earth your thoughts create and become reality. I will say your world is like a world of frozen thought. It takes longer to create form, and for some of you, even longer to let it go. Because time on this plane is slow, you must practice economy of energy, and that is one of the reasons it may seem to take so long to create what you want.

If you focus on having something, you can go straight to it with purpose. It may still be a matter of years before you reach your goals, but having a higher purpose saves time. When you live your higher purpose, you compress time, accelerate your evolution into becoming your soul, and raise your vibration. The more you know your purpose, the less you waste energy, and the faster you can go higher.

Ultimately, higher purpose is spiritual evolution. The new home, the finished project, is not the goal of growth. The process by which you create these things and the growth it gives you — the new skills you acquire, the insights, the opening of your heart when you love, the new appreciation for beauty your garden gives you when flowers or crops come up, the feelings you have when you finish a project, the focus and concentration when you work — this is higher purpose, this is evolution.

*Spiritual growth means
increasing your awareness of
beauty, opening your heart,
and experiencing more love
and compassion.*

When I speak of higher purpose, I am speaking of soul-purpose, which means balancing all your energies and harmonizing your being with your soul's note. Each one of you has a soul sound, a note; the more you can express it outwardly into the world through your voice, the more you can create forms in the outer world that match your inner being. You can start by letting sounds come out of your mouth, until you find a beautiful, comfortable sound. You will notice that as you sound your note, you begin breathing more deeply and rhythmically. This will assist you in clearing your aura and raising your vibration, just to sound beautiful, comfortable notes. This process will harmonize the various parts of your being.

Evolution occurs in many ways depending on where you are on your path. Ultimately, souls start out on earth in the denser energies and work their way up into the higher and finer energies. Some of you move into higher and finer energies very quickly, while others take longer. What are some of the things that make it take longer to grow? One is the inability to let go of form when there is no essence behind it. When the reason for a form you created is gone, it is time to let it go. You have seen this in relationships, with those who hang on to the shell of a relationship when the life energy has gone out of the connection.

Another thing that slows your evolution is lack of purpose. If you are looking upward, intending to go higher, then you will, if that is your purpose. You can then take every situation in your life and ask, "Does this evolve and bring me higher, or does it not?" If it does not, you can ask again, "Is there any way I can change this situation or be with this person in such a way that I can grow?"

You can find and live in higher purpose no matter what situation you are in. You can come out of the denser energies of heavy emotions, fear, or pain. The earth plane can be a beautiful place to experience. The ability to enjoy the senses, to hear sounds, touch, feel, and know love, can lead to joyous experiences. You *can* come out of separateness. In so many ways you create separateness and loneliness. In your Universe you not only have individual bodies but you so often feel separated from your own true self. For instance, every time you have a doubt, thinking you are not good or strong enough, you have created separation from your higher self. The path of your soul is to join together all your parts and merge with your higher self.

You can also talk of purpose in terms of the concrete things you wish to accomplish. I would recommend first that you ask, "What is the essence behind the form?" For instance, if you want to start a business, what is its highest purpose? How does it serve the planet? How does it serve you? If you want to reach a financial goal, you can first ask, what is the essence of that goal? How do I serve my higher purpose by creating that form? If you want money to get your work out into the world to create a project that will heal others, if you simply want to be a vehicle for healing (not for egotistical reasons), then the Universe will send you money in abundance. Anything you seek to possess or hold on to will slow down your growth. The Universe, in its loving, gentle way, will seek to prevent you from having it, or it will leave on its own. If you still have things you are hanging on to long after they are of use to you, you will find yourself living in a harder, heavier energy, one of more struggle.

Life need not be hard.

You can create joy by softening your energy. What do I mean by softening? Whenever people are mad at you, you can easily respond with anger and hardness. On the other hand, you can soften so much that you look at them with deep compassion. This separates your energy from theirs at the personality level and connects you in the heart.

Many of you think that you need to have great willpower and control over your energy. If you are living with purpose, you will find you are also living in harmony with your energy, not needing to control it. On a concrete level, this means not spending idle time, even in your mind, and resisting the temptation to go over past situations that did not bring you joy. Again, sounding your note, singing, is a way to bring yourself back to center. Notice your mind becoming clearer and freer when you do so. The more you sound your note, the more you will find one that feels in harmony with your being. It is not something that can be taught, but is something that you must find for yourself. It is a joyful, comfortable, peaceful sound, and you always feel better afterward.

Before you were born, you did not decide *how*, you simply decided what energies you would evolve within yourself. The things that happen, the careers you choose, the people you attract are simply the effect of your evolution. They are the creation and the product of it. You may be confused, thinking that a new house or relationship marks your progress. In one way they do, but you have already made progress, long before these things came into your life.

Go inward for a moment, feel your energy, and allow a picture, symbol, image, feeling, or word to come that represents your purpose here. What is your growth centering on in this lifetime? What have been your main challenges? What, in form, have you wanted to create in your outer world?

Higher purpose is always something you love.

In the next month, become more aware of your purpose. It is always playful and joyful. Higher purpose leads to the finer energies of life, such as a deep connection with a loved one, the joyful union of friends as they play, and the lightness as you carry out your life work. Joy can exist in every moment if you are willing to live in purpose.

Manifesting higher purpose means believing in yourself and believing in the goodness of the Universe. If you were to make one decision that would assist you most in manifesting higher purpose, it would be to believe in yourself and to trust the Universe. From my perspective, there is so much love, there are so many people within twenty miles of your home you could connect with in a loving way, and there is such an abundance of money in your society that you can realize any purpose you choose.

A way to create your life purpose is to connect with your inner self and bring this self out to the world through your words and actions. This life gives you an opportunity to live in more light and to live joyfully. Whatever you achieve by the time you die is yours. Every gain you make, every place in your life where you insert love and joy, every place you find laughter, peace, and delight, will already be present in your next lifetime, wherever you may be. Every time you evolve your body, eat in a better way, exercise more, dance, play, focus, and bring in light, you evolve in future lifetimes also. Part of the purpose of earth life is to bring in your higher self and join with your spirit, your innermost being, at all levels. Each one of you has the ability to help and heal others, and most of you have a sincere desire to do so.

Wake up in the morning and hold your higher purpose in your hands as a symbol. Imagine that you are holding in your hands the highest purpose you came to create in this lifetime. Bring it into your heart. Pour light into it; ask for guidance and assistance from the higher forces. Feel your energy going upward and let go of it so that it may come back to you. Holding that purpose in your heart, you refine your physical body, raise your thoughts upward, and bring peace to your emotions. How would it feel if every cell in your body acknowledged and was in touch with your higher purpose?

Doing this is so powerful that it will be effective even done as little as once a year. You are sending a message to the Universe telling it you are willing to grow. The Universe will then bring you many opportunities to expand and evolve, and none of your challenges will ever be beyond that which you have the skills and tools to handle. Earth can be a very gentle place. However, in some of the coarser and denser levels of energy, it may not feel so gentle.

You learn and grow
from everything you create.

If you are experiencing a crisis in your life, it may be because experiencing a crisis draws you closer to your soul.

Crises can happen when you are off course in some area of your life as a way to bring you back in touch with your soul and its higher purpose. Crises often result in your reaching inward and upward to connect with your soul, so you can bring about solutions from a higher level. If you are willing to live in higher purpose, listen to yourself, connect with your soul, and take action on its whispers, you will not have to create crisis or struggle. You do not even need to know the form of your purpose, but only have the intent to create higher purpose to bring it to you. Purpose represents movement of the soul, the energy that connects heaven and earth. It is marked by concrete forms — a new house, a marriage, those things that you have been seeking. Those are only the outer forms that mark new growth in the soul. Because you are growing, all of you, so rapidly, you must create new challenges to experience who you are. These can be joyful opportunities in the higher realms, or they can become crisis and struggle in the lower realms.

If you want to live in higher purpose, begin making it more of a commitment. How do you spend your time? Where do your thoughts go when you are alone? Learn to hold a higher focus, to spend time thinking of why you are here and what you have to offer humanity. Purpose comes through serving the higher self, assisting others, and being willing to carry out your vision of the highest service you can offer. Think of something you can do this week, something specific that you know to be part of your higher purpose, be it a short-term or long-term purpose you are serving. Be willing to acknowledge, when you have taken this step, that you are living in higher purpose. When you complete it, you can create the next new thing to do to live in higher purpose.

As you go through your day, tell yourself what a beautiful person you are. See the beauty in yourself. Feel your inner strength, acknowledge how good and loving you are. Sense all the light around you. Acknowledge yourself, and as you do so, look for your higher purpose. You know what you want to do next. You may have reasons why you cannot do it, old memories and patterns that seem to stop you, but you do know what you want. Bring it up to the surface, pull it up from the unconscious, from the whispers in your mind, and make it real. Hold your vision in front of you. If you want a peaceful and quiet life, to be a good parent, to have a man or woman in your life who loves and values and treasures you, bring up that vision. Make a decision and you will have it.

Get clear on your intent. If you want to serve the world and get your work out, if you want to create prosperity, to open to new creativity and skills, there is always a part of you that knows how. Talk to that part, ask it to show you what steps to take. Watch your inner dialogue, and listen for messages from this part.

Manifesting is a matter of trusting and believing in yourself and of steadily holding your vision of what you want to create. There are many temptations to stop believing and trusting in the Universe and yourself, but there are many reasons to continue. The Universe often tests you to see how much you believe in your vision. Every goal is reachable if you keep working on it.

Living in Higher Purpose
PLAYSHEET

1. Sounding your soul's note infuses you with your soul's qualities of higher purpose, light, love, power, energy, clarity, peace, balance, and joy. Imagine you are linking with your soul right now and inwardly sounding your soul's note. As you do, picture these soul qualities flowing into you, becoming who you are, strengthening you in every way.

2. As you sound your soul's note, allow your heart to open. You can express your soul's higher purpose through love. Picture radiating your soul's note of love and compassion to your friends, loved ones, activities, circumstances; to your thoughts, emotions, and body. Radiate love to the animal, vegetable, and mineral kingdoms and to the earth itself if you choose.

3. Think of one specific way you can express your soul's higher purpose now. Aligned with your soul's note of love and higher purpose, ask yourself:

   - How does expressing my soul's higher purpose in this way bring more light, joy, and harmony into my life?
   - How does it bring more light, joy, and harmony into others' lives?
   - How does creating this goal serve humanity?

4. What one step, however small, could you take toward expressing your soul's higher purpose in this way?

DAILY JOY PRACTICE

Today you can choose to accelerate your spiritual growth and create those things that serve your own and humanity's evolution by focusing on your higher purpose. Set your intention to live in higher purpose today. As you think of the day ahead, imagine being aware of your higher purpose throughout the day. One way to increase your awareness of your higher purpose is to stop often throughout the day, such as when you finish one activity or interaction and before you start the next, and ask your soul, "What is my higher purpose now?"

As you ask this question, your innermost self will send you energy and guidance about what to do next. All you need do is be open and receptive to whatever comes into your mind or happens after that. Perhaps you will have a new, creative idea, or someone will come to you with something he or she needs done. Trust that whatever happens next is the response of your soul and the Universe to your question, "What is my higher purpose right now?"

At the end of the day, reflect back on how your day was different as you focused on your higher purpose. Did you change any of your activities? Did you do anything in a new or different way? How do you feel about the day? How often did you remember to ask for guidance about your higher purpose? Did anything unusual happen as you did this?

When you focus on living in higher purpose, you are in harmony with the Universe. Doors open; synchronicity happens. You are in the flow where things happen easily and joyfully. As you align with the purpose of your soul and allow that purpose to be expressed in your thoughts, words, and activities, you will rapidly evolve in this lifetime.

AFFIRMATIONS

I accelerate my spiritual growth by living in higher purpose.

I express my higher purpose in all that I do.

I am living in higher purpose right now as I read
and say these affirmations.

I follow my heart and do what I love
from moment to moment.

My soul is bringing me everything I need
to fulfill my purpose.

I open my heart. I experience more love
and compassion every day.

I appreciate all the beauty in my life.

Things happen easily and joyfully in my life.

I am sounding my soul's note through my voice
with every word I speak.

I do those things that evolve, inspire,
and lift others and me higher.

I am living my higher purpose as I do what I love.

I check in often with my innermost self to know
and live my higher purpose.

I believe in myself and in the goodness of the Universe.

I align every cell in my body with my higher purpose.

I am committed to living in higher purpose.

I trust my inner guidance.

I now live in higher purpose.

I am one with my soul and spirit.

I am one with the Universe.

CHAPTER EIGHTEEN

Recognizing Life Purpose: What Are You Here to Do?

Many of you are in a state of transition. States of transition always create much energy. Whether you are feeling high or low, you certainly feel alive, full of spirit and energy, whenever your life is changing. That strong part of you, the part that is able to detach and observe, that is looking at the light, that wants your life to be better, more joyful, and more peaceful, comes out at these times.

What are you here to do? Recognizing life purpose enables you to manifest your destiny. Do not get me wrong; you are free beings. You did not set out a course before you were born that you *had* to follow. You laid some groundwork, provided yourself with certain parents, and chose to be born in a certain part of the world. You set up circumstances for your life so you would be aimed like a projectile in a certain direction. Once you are here, your life is spontaneous and decided upon from moment to moment. There is no predetermined limit to how high you can go. There are no limits!

*You live in a limitless world;
you can expand beyond
anything you know.*

To look at your life purpose, look beyond the mass thoughtforms that exist. Many of you have grown up with a great deal of pressure to do, to accomplish, and to be, to make a name for yourselves, to feel worthy in one way or another. When you look at life purpose, ask your soul and yourself, "Am I doing this for me, for my highest good, or am I doing it to please others, to live up to their image of me? Am I accomplishing this purpose so that I may receive a pat on the back or recognition? Or am I doing it because it is something I want to do, that fits who I am, and that brings me joy?"

I see so many expectations and beliefs in your culture about being a good and valuable person — such as making a lot of money, or being well known, or being quite spiritual and pious. All of these things can be good if they come from your soul and are part of your higher path. These things can be off your path if you are doing them only to fulfill an image that comes from the ego or personality. Look at yourself right now and ask, if society had no images it held up and admired as being good or right, what would you do with your life? There has been an emphasis on outer productivity in your culture rather than on inner peace, joy, love, and compassion. There is a sense of *time* that pervades everything — accomplish this or that by the age of such and such or be considered a failure. There is a sense of pressure, that everything must be done fast. You have all the time you need to accomplish things that are part of your life purpose.

You can relax and know that as you go through each day, you have the time to accomplish your purpose. If you do not feel you are accomplishing your purpose, that you do not have enough time, then I will say that what you are doing is probably not your purpose. When you are creating your life purpose, you will have enough time, for you will create the time. You will find it so joyful that everything else falls away, and your determination, focus, and concentration *are* there. If there is anything you are forcing yourself to do out of duty or obligation, out of feeling that people will admire you or respect you when you do it, then you are probably not honoring the light of your soul.

Each one of you has a different purpose, and you cannot judge others by what you see them doing. Each one of you has set out to learn certain things in this lifetime, to grow in every way possible. Many of the blocks to manifesting life purpose come from the cultural mass thoughtforms, a lack of training, and other people, particularly those close to you. In a close personal relationship, people tend to take on the goals and the thoughtforms of the other. As you look at your life purpose, look at who you are close to in your life, and ask, have you been manifesting what they wanted for you? Are you clear about what you want for yourself? Often those who love you the most can be the ones who most hold you back — not through their negativity, but through their idea of love, through their wanting what they think is best for you, or their wanting you to be there for them, or to live up to their pictures and goals for your life.

As you look at your life purpose, ask, what would you do if you were alone? If no one in your life would gain or lose from what you did, would it change your choices? What would *you* do for yourself? What would bring you peace and joy? What if society did not exist or had absolutely different values — would you still love what you are doing? A hundred years ago, many values were different. People were admired for many things that are no longer valued. Society's beliefs are changing and fluid, and if you base your actions on what you see around you, those actions will not necessarily reflect your higher purpose.

Imagine that you are a rock in a stream and the stream is moving all around you. Now, many of you let the stream carry you this way or that. Do you stay centered and balanced while the current flows by, or do you let every current throw you around?

Imagine you have an antenna in your mind, and you can adjust it right now, aiming it upward, to the higher ideals that fit you. What do you value in yourself? How do you want to feel? Stop for one moment and ask, what feelings do I want? How do I want my Universe to look right now? On an emotional level, bring those feelings to yourself as if right now at this moment you had your perfect Universe. Keep this antenna adjusted upward to higher levels of the Universe, and you will be stable like the rock, while all the currents flow by you.

> *It is only an illusion*
> *that you do not have*
> *what you want.*

If you believe in what you see, then you are believing in the creations of the past. Everything you have right now in your life you created from the past. Everything you have from here on out can be created at this moment, and it can be created differently. You do not need to know specifically what you will do today or the next day. You can start by *believing* that you do have a purpose, a concrete purpose, and you can begin by asking it to unfold for you. If you begin believing in and acting as if you know what to do with your life, you will. Pretend today that you are the captain of your ship, and that for today you will guide this ship the way you want to. You will take the time you need, be with the people you want to be with, say "no" when you want to say no, and "yes" when you want to say yes. You will check in from hour to hour to see if you are feeling joy or peace or whatever you have determined that you want to feel.

Some say their life purpose is serving and assisting others. This can be a very good and true life purpose if you also pay attention to making your own life work. By taking care of *you*, putting yourself in an environment that increases your sense of peace and serenity, beauty and harmony, you are in a much better position to assist others than if you put the focus on making them happy and yet are not happy yourself. If every person came from a space of harmony and beauty, of the higher self and soul, you would have an entirely different society. Right now, look around at all of your options and choices. Decide that from today onward you will create the world that you want. Go within and find that point of strength, that part of you that has always been able to create the things you wanted, and feel it growing stronger. The greatest gift you give another is having your own life work.

Life changes and transitions are often preceded by confusion, by a sense of loss or pain, or by a sense that things are falling apart. That is because there is little training in your society about letting go and detaching from forms that are no longer appropriate. There is a mass thoughtform of scarcity, which makes it even harder to let go, thinking there will be nothing better to replace what you are losing. If you focus on what you want, if you acknowledge that what you have is a creation of the past that you can easily change, your future can look any way you choose.

Fill your thoughts with what you want to create, and you will have it.

There is usually a time lag between the thought about what you want to create and the time that it takes to appear in your life. This time lag confuses and stops many people from continuing to think of new things they want to create. Thoughts are real and go outward to create what they represent, and thoughts exist in time. Past thoughts may still affect you for a while, even as you change your thinking. Within two to three months, however, the new thoughts will have gained momentum and will start to create new outer forms and circumstances to match.

Honor yourself as a unique individual. When you are with other people, do not compare your path to theirs. Often you compare what they are doing with their lives to what you are doing with yours, and you feel you are better than or less than them. Instead, go inward and look at what your highest path is, and compare your life to that. You read stories in the newspapers about things that happen to other people, and you may think, "This may happen to me." You do not have their thoughts; you are not them. Whatever happens to others happens because of who they are, their beliefs and thoughts. If you hear other people's stories, do not bring them into your space and internalize them, but ask yourself, "How can

I be true to who I am? What is *my* truth?" Every person has a different path and is a unique expression of life force.

> *Life purpose is whatever path*
> *you decide on,*
> *for all is free will.*

Prior to being born, your soul sets up those conditions that would best allow you throughout your life to unfold certain qualities, skills, and life directions. You can have what you want, if you are willing to hold up the vision and believe in yourself consistently. The more consistently you believe in yourself, the better the results. It would be easy if there were no setbacks (as you interpret them) or trials along the way. Honor every seeming setback, every single challenge or difficulty, for it strengthens your purpose. It gives you opportunities to be even more committed to your vision, even clearer on your intent. If life were too easy or simple, most of you would be complaining of boredom. Honor your challenges, for those spaces that you label as dark are actually there to strengthen you, to firm your resolve, and to bring out the best in you.

Recognizing Life Purpose
Playsheet

1. Believe that you do have a life purpose, and ask that it unfold for you. One way to do so is to close your eyes and allow a picture, symbol, or image to come to mind that represents your purpose here on earth.

2. Bring your symbol into your heart. Ask your soul and the higher forces of the Universe to breathe more light and life into it. Imagine your symbol changing color, texture, and size. Whenever you are uncertain about your life purpose, think about and interact with this symbol.

3. Acknowledge that you are the captain of your ship. You are guiding the ship of your life the way you want to, knowing that as you do what you love and are guided to do, you are living your life purpose.

4. Think about your life. Knowing that you are living your life purpose as you do what you want with your life, answer the following questions:

   • What activities would you let go of that do not bring you a sense of aliveness?
   • What activities would you bring into your life that you would love to do?
   • What relationships would you change, and how would you change them?
   • What else would you change about your life?

DAILY JOY PRACTICE

Today, if you choose, commit to recognizing your life purpose in new and broader ways. With this intention, imagine you are connecting with your soul and the higher forces of the Universe. Affirm that you are ready to know more about your life purpose and your next steps. Decide you are open to receiving all the love and assistance that is available to you.

As you request assistance in recognizing your life purpose and what you are here to do, sense the light of your soul's purpose becoming visible to you, calling you forward and drawing your attention upward. Allow this light of life purpose to illuminate your entire being. Receive it into every part of your body, emotions, and mind. Affirm that you will recognize and be aware of your life purpose as it appears throughout the day in the relationships, activities, and opportunities that present themselves.

Ask for the light of purpose to shine through you and dissolve all unnecessary activities, busyness, and situations that are not your purpose. As the light of purpose becomes stronger and more visible to you, distractions will fall away. There will be special moments when a higher vision emerges, showing you the more joyful, loving, and peaceful reality that awaits you.

As you become more aware of your life purpose and as your purpose guides your actions and words, everything in your life will change for the better. Your activities and goals, your relationships, thoughts, and desires will be transformed. Embrace now all that you can be and all that you are!

AFFIRMATIONS

My life is unfolding in perfect ways.

There are no limits to how high I can go.

I live in a limitless world.

I am true to myself. I say "no" when I mean no,
and "yes" when I mean yes.

My life purpose illuminates my life and shows me the way.

My life purpose guides me in all that I do.

I release anything that stands in the way
of living my life purpose.

I am now living my life purpose.

My life is growing better every day.

All that I need is within me.
I am living my greatest potential.

My inner vision is clear. I know who I am.

Everything I do is something I want to do,
fits who I am, and brings me joy.

I have all the time I need to accomplish my life purpose.

I have the determination and focus
I need to create my life purpose.

I choose to be in an environment that increases
my sense of aliveness, peace, and joy, and I am!

My life works in wonderful ways.

I know all challenges are in my life to bring
out the best in me.

I embrace all that I am and all that I can be.

Stories from Our Readers

I want to share a few of the stories people have written to me about their experiences with *Living with Joy*. My hope is that these stories will inspire you and help you to discover all the ways that you can put the principles and practices in this book to work in your life.

One of Orin's main teachings in *Living with Joy* is that we can learn to grow through joy rather than through pain, struggle, or crisis. As one woman wrote, "Seven years ago I came across the book *Living with Joy* and I fell in love with it. I fell in love with the idea that I could and should be happy and that I could grow with joy. I have read it often for many years, and I am experiencing more joy and positive energy. It is my all-time favorite book." Another man wrote about his definite decision to let go of pain and struggle in his insightful note: "I want to say that Orin's teachings on how to stop thinking about things that bother you have helped me so much. I had never given myself permission to simply STOP thinking about things that were making me sad or angry, and now I can do this. I feel so much better."

I could feel one man's wonderfully open heart, and all the gifts he would have to offer his new son, as I read from him: "Hello, I am currently an English teacher, a husband, and new father who meditates almost every morning and a little before bed. I have studied and read fairly regularly from *Living with Joy*. I find that the messages there sit in the 'back' of my consciousness and echo when I encounter situations or difficulties in life. The books have truly helped me to raise my life's vibration, which is an invaluable gift, better than anything I can imagine. I like to read the books over and over again. They are very stimulating and I can feel love washing over me as I read and immediately afterward."

Living with Joy *can assist you if you are experiencing challenges or going through a difficult time.*

If you are experiencing difficulties, or feel you need more confidence, self-love, or hope about a better future, you will find much guidance and support in this book. Many wrote that *Living with Joy* got them through a crisis by helping them to feel more confident and peaceful. As one woman triumphantly wrote, "Ten years ago I hit rock bottom when I lost everything in this world in the space of two months. My house burned down, I had a miscarriage, and my partner left me. I happened to come across your book, *Living with Joy*, and it reminded me I could handle anything. I turned my life around after reading this book." Practicing the principles taught in *Living with Joy* can help you face with more confidence whatever challenges are in your life.

One person thankfully noted, "A friend lent me *Living with Joy* after an extremely upsetting breakup of a long-term relationship, as well as many other changes that happened at this time. I was in deep distress. *Living with Joy* helped me understand I was not happy where I had been and that the Universe was trying to steer me onto my right path. The book changed my perceptions and my life. I could not let my friend have the book back until I got my own copy!"

Living with Joy *can change your outlook on life to one that supports you in feeling good about yourself.*

People found that *Living with Joy* changed their outlook on life, no matter what kind of challenges or difficulties they were experiencing. Some people were having relationship problems, some had financial difficulties, had lost a job, or were dealing with a health issue, either their own or that of a loved one. They wrote to tell of various challenges and problems that had turned around after reading *Living with Joy*.

One woman bravely wrote from the hospital, "The books have changed me and my life to a new, more loving and positive person. I have a new improved life now. All I have learned from the books saved me in the most difficult period of my life since an illness and the hard and painful treatments I am going through. Orin's guidance has a great positive influence on me. It also helps my family to change their point of view and to see the bright side of life even in the midst of difficulties. My family and I are grateful for all the important advice and guidance provided in your books, not only *Living with Joy* but in all of Orin's books."

Another man touchingly wrote, "It is amazing how safe Orin's books make you feel, especially *Living with Joy*, and how much they help in times of difficulties. I am twenty-four years old, recently lost my mother and grandmother, and am now accompanying my terminally ill father. It is a very difficult time for me, and this book has given me strength and helped me keep faith in life and faith in myself. I now know I can help with visualization, sending light, even in situations when others would think there is no hope. This has helped me and relieved me so much! Orin's books are dense in information and practice, offering many things to do to grow. I can read them over and over again, and I still feel like I am learning new things, understanding better, and consolidating my knowledge."

One woman's experience moved me. She wrote, "I first came upon *Living with Joy* years ago. The book had been given to one of my friends who was dying of cancer, and I started to read it while I attended her (she was sleeping) and became totally absorbed in it. Through that book, Orin spoke to me directly, and the images he conjured up were as clear as if I had been watching television or a movie. My dying friend gave me the book, one of the most important gifts I have ever received, and I have read it many times since."

Another man shared his hope and newfound strength, writing, "The last few years have been very difficult. *Living with Joy* has given me the strength and the knowledge that I needed to get myself through these particularly trying times. I lost my job and have been feeling very negative about the world. *Living with Joy* has shown me that there is hope, and that I can love and appreciate myself and feel positive about my life without needing outer things to change. And, my life is changing already for the better since reading this book."

Living with Joy *can assist you in being true to yourself.*

Some people wrote to say that they had felt different all their lives about their beliefs and feelings. They felt they had to put on an appearance for other people. Reading *Living with*

Joy made them feel better about themselves — more confident, self-assured, and able to honor their feelings around others. As one man shared, "Orin's books speak directly to me, offering me what I need to hear, to know, and desire most in life. I have felt alone in most of my beliefs and have never really found anyone to share this beauty with. These books contain what I seem to have always known, and then I have moments of forgetfulness. Orin has helped me to move forward and remember who I am."

I could feel the relief and gratitude from another woman who wrote, "I am currently reading *Living with Joy*. My heart is filled with tears of joy as I read each and every page. It feels as though Orin is speaking directly to ME. I have been searching for a way to love myself for a long time. I have been so lost, and I don't feel lost anymore."

Living with Joy *can assist you in feeling more positive about your day, your life, and your relationships.*

I often received stories from people about how much more positive and enjoyable their life has become after practicing what they learned in this book. One woman's email was filled with joy as she stated, "I enjoy reading *Living with Joy* at the beach on the weekends. I feel energized, connected, and happy every time I have this book in my hands." Others wrote that this book not only made their own lives better, but they also became a positive influence on those around them.

One man expressed surprise at all the changes he experienced and how easy it was to make them. He wrote, "I've been reading *Living with Joy*, and I must admit that this book has made me rethink many/most of my views and opinions. So now, I am trying to change the working mode of my mind into positive thinking. It takes some exercise though. However, it is easier than what I have anticipated. Many problems I used to have suddenly disappeared. All of a sudden I've become an optimist. My friends can't believe the changes they see in me and ask me what I am doing. They like being around me."

Another woman enjoyed sharing the following: "I've currently read *Living with Joy*, and it has been a very positive impact in my life. I noticed that once I started really reading it, listening to the messages in it, and doing the journal exercises, I had more positive things come into my life. I talked about it so much to a coworker, she ended up going out and buying the book as well. I revisit the book when I feel things stressing me out or getting me down."

You can experience practical and immediate results as you follow the principles in this book.

Many people wrote to share with me inspiring stories of how they had experienced many practical results and immediate changes from working with the principles taught by Orin in this book. You may experience many practical results yourself, such as those one reader described: "I am experiencing tremendous changes since practicing what is in the *Living with Joy* book. I am seeing many practical results. I love the new me! Things that I never thought possible are happening to me." As one reader shared, "I bought *Living with Joy*, and reading it was an uplifting experience in itself. Orin's words really helped raise my vibration. I could tell the difference right away. I am now reading it a second time."

You can positively affect everyone around you.

Many people who wrote told us that they loved *Living with Joy* so much they read all three of Orin's Earth Life books. As one person wrote, "I have been reading *Living with Joy*,

Personal Power through Awareness, and *Spiritual Growth* over and over. I can't put them down and have highly recommended them to other people. I have been on my path for nearly seven years now and have noticed and felt a tremendous difference in myself. I am calmer (people have also told me that I have a calming effect on them). I experience inner peace, tranquility, joy, happiness and have opened my heart more, which I am still working on, as well as setting boundaries. I am also working on keeping in balance when around negative or low energies, which has been a challenge for me. I have evolved and grown a great deal in seven years as I continue to strive to become my Higher Self."

One woman wrote joyfully of her transformation since reading the books: "Hello and thank you first of all for your courage and guidance in putting your materials out there for us to learn and grow from. I was advised by my counselor to read *Living with Joy.* I was so moved and my life changed so drastically that I eagerly purchased *Personal Power through Awareness* and *Spiritual Growth.* As I have read these books I feel I am a new person and that I have found the missing link I always knew was out there. I am so much closer to knowing who I am and why I am here that I had to write and share this with you. Orin has transformed me and my life, and it is slowly spreading to all the people in my realm that I am helping and sending love to."

I love hearing from you and thank you for your comments.

I find your notes, letters, and emails inspiring, and appreciate hearing about your courage, inner strength, and determination to create a more fulfilling life and to experience more love and joy in your life. As you read this book, you too can look forward to many of the changes people wrote about, such as, "This book has helped me gain insight and given me hope. It changed my thinking and therefore my life." "I read and studied *Living with Joy* and it turned my life completely around." "*Living with Joy* set me on a whole new path in life and for this I am profoundly grateful." "I read the *Living with Joy* book and I found it very helpful, encouraging, and applicable to just about all matters in my life. I find it is so supportive and reassuring as I change my negatives into positives."

All of you who are reading this book and changing your lives are making a contribution to planetary consciousness. As you commit to living a more joyful, peaceful, harmonious, loving, and fulfilling life, you are making that choice more available to everyone. You are helping to shift the world thoughtform of growing through crisis and struggle into one of growing through joy, peace, and love. Affirm, if you choose, that you are ready now to grow through joy rather than through struggle, crisis, or pain. Know that as you do you are not only changing your own life for the better, but you are also opening the way for all those who are following one step behind you, who are seeking and looking for a way to change their lives for the better.

Acknowledgments

From my heart I want to thank Orin for his unending patience, guidance, and wisdom.

I want to especially thank all of you who are reading and working with *Living with Joy* for the light you are adding to the world as you open to living and growing through joy, love, and peace. Your stories touch my heart. You are opening the door for everyone who is one step behind, so that they, too, may experience a wonderful and joyful life.

I want to express my deep gratitude to Hal and Linda Kramer for their friendship and for their ongoing support of Orin's work in publishing these books. I am very grateful to New World Library for their ongoing support of Orin's books. For their support in creating this *Living with Joy* anniversary edition, I especially want to thank Marc Allen, publisher; Georgia Hughes, editorial director; Munro Magruder, associate publisher; Kristen Cashman, managing editor; Tona Pearce Myers, production director; Jonathan Wichmann, editorial assistant;

Mary Ann Casler, cover designer; and Jeff Campbell, freelance copyeditor.

I want to extend my gratitude to those who helped us organize Orin's material and put it into this form: Ginny Porter, for her many hours of work with me on this book revision; Edward Alpern, for his years of dedicated work with Orin; LaUna Huffines, for her many contributions to the original *Living with Joy* book; Trisha Studer, for managing the LuminEssence office; Mitch Posada, for his beautiful art and graphics; and Marty Piter, for his audio engineer work on all of Orin's audio programs, assisted by Greg Badger.

With deep gratitude, I thank all the distributors and their staffs, as well as all the committed, dedicated bookstore owners, and those who make Orin's books available through their websites and online stores — all of whom make it possible for Orin's books to reach you. I also want to thank our international publishers, who have produced this book in over twenty-four languages, making this information available around the world.

Companion Books

All books are available in printed form; and in Kindle and ePub eBook formats; and as Audiobooks read by Sanaya Roman, or Sanaya Roman and Duane Packer for the *Opening to Channel* Audiobook.

By Orin
BOOK 2 OF THE EARTH LIFE SERIES

Personal Power Through Awareness
A Guidebook for Sensitive People
By Sanaya Roman

This is an accelerated, step-by-step course in sensing energy. Using these easy-to-follow processes, thousands have learned to create immediate and profound changes in their relationships, self-image, and ability to love and be loved. You need no longer be affected by other people's moods or negativity. You can recognize when you have taken on other people's energy and easily release it. You can learn to stay centered and balanced, know who you are, increase the positive energy around you, and love and help others. Your sensitivity is a gift. Learn to use it to send and receive telepathic messages, increase your intuitive abilities, and open to higher guidance. You can leave the denser energies, where things are often painful, and live in the higher energies where you can feel loving, calm, focused, and positive. PPTA (H J Kramer, Inc, 216 pages)

BOOK 3 OF THE EARTH LIFE SERIES

Spiritual Growth: *Being Your Higher Self*
By Sanaya Roman

This book will teach you how to reach upward and work with the higher powers of the universe to accelerate your spiritual growth. You will learn how to link with the Higher Will to flow with the universe; connect with the Universal Mind for insights, enhanced creativity, and breakthroughs; expand your awareness of the inner planes; open your clairvoyant sight; receive revelations; and see the bigger picture of the universe. You will learn non-attachment, right use of will, and how to lift the veils of illusion. You will learn how to expand and contract time, choose your reality, become transparent, communicate in higher ways, and be your higher self. These tools will help you live your everyday life with more joy, harmony, peace, and love. This book will help you align with the higher energies that are coming, using them to live the best life you can imagine for yourself. SG (H J Kramer, Inc, 252 pages)

LuminEssence Productions • www.orindaben.com

Soul Love: Awakening Your Heart Centers
By Sanaya Roman

In *Soul Love*, Orin's first book of the Soul Life Series, you will meet and blend with your soul. You will learn more about your chakras and how to work with your soul and the Beings of Light to awaken your heart centers. When these centers are awakened and working together in a triangle of light, you can more easily experience soul love, peace, joy, bliss, and aliveness. Discover how to attract a soul mate, soul link, make heart connections, create soul relationships, change personality love into soul love, and lift all the energies about you into your heart center to be purified and transformed. See results in your life when you use Orin's easy, step-by-step processes to heal your heart of past hurts, to open to receive more love, and to bring all your relationships to a higher level. SL (H J Kramer, Inc, 252 pages)

By Orin and DaBen

Opening to Channel: How to Connect With Your Guide
By Sanaya Roman and Duane Packer

Orin and DaBen–a wise and healing spirit teacher channeled by Duane Packer–will teach you how to connect with and verbally channel a high-level guide. Channeling is a skill that can be learned, and Sanaya and Duane have successfully trained thousands to channel using these safe, simple, and effective processes. You will learn what channeling is and how to know if you are ready to channel, go into trance, receive information clearly, what to expect in your first meeting with your guide, and much more. OTC (H J Kramer, Inc, 264 pages)

Creating Money: Attracting Abundance
By Sanaya Roman and Duane Packer

Learn how to follow the spiritual laws of abundance, use advanced manifesting techniques, and create what you want. Learn how to draw your life's work to you. This book contains many simple techniques, positive affirmations, and exercises to help you create rapid changes in your prosperity. Abundance is your natural state, and you can learn how to let money and abundance flow readily into your life while doing what you love. You can develop unlimited thinking, listen to your inner guidance, and transform your beliefs. Discover how to work with energy to easily create what you want and tap into the unlimited abundance of the universe. CM (H J Kramer Inc with New World Library, 288 pages)

Living with Joy Audio Courses

Living with Joy Audio Albums by Orin

The *Living with Joy* guided meditations by Orin in Parts 1 and 2 will help you practice the techniques in this book as well as teach you new skills of how to live with joy. These *Living with Joy* audio courses will assist you in bringing joy into your life on a daily basis. You can experience new levels of peace, joy, clarity, harmony, love, balance, and other qualities of your soul as you listen to these guided meditations. You will be guided to look at your life from a higher perspective. You will learn to grow through joy and release struggle and limitation. As you work with this course, you can experience more self-love and radiate unconditional love to others.

Part 1: Living with Joy. Includes: *Finding Your Path of Joy; Changing Negatives into Positives; The Art of Self-Love, Self-Worth and Self-Esteem; Power: Refining Your Ego; Knowing Your Heart's Wisdom; Opening to Receive;* and *Appreciation and Gratitude.* 8 meditations by Orin with beautiful music by Thaddeus. *(L201)*

Part 2: Taking a Quantum Leap. Includes: *Finding Inner Peace; Balance and Stability; Clarity: Living in the Light; Freedom; Embracing the New; Taking a Quantum Leap; Living in Higher Purpose; Recognizing Life Purpose.* 8 meditations by Orin with music by Thaddeus. *(L202)*

Living with Joy Affirmations and Guided Meditation
Program 1 is a guided meditation based on the book's principles. Program 2 contains some of the affirmations from this book. (L100)

Visit our website or contact LuminEssence for ordering information, media formats available, and cost.

Free Orin Newsletters and eNewsletters

Visit our website, sign our guestbook, and let us know about yourself. Read our free newsletter containing information about Orin's audio courses, books, articles, and affirmations to assist you in living with joy. We offer "eNewsletters" sent to you several times a year (not the same as our printed newsletter) if we have your email address. These contain links to free Orin audio meditations and articles. These are Orin's way of continuing to assist you with your growth by providing you with information, processes, and his transmissions of energy. We have many free offerings on our website; see last page of this book for more information.

Orin Audio Meditations

A Message from Orin About These Guided Meditations

"I offer these audio meditations to you who have read my books and want to go further, using and living these principles. Working with guided meditations, where your mind is in a relaxed, open state, is a powerful way to create rapid, profound, and lasting changes in your life." – *Orin*

Single Guided Meditations

Living with Joy Affirmations and Guided Journey *(L100)*
 Based on the book's principles.
Feeling Inner Peace *(L101)* Self-Love *(L102)* Opening to Receive *(L106)*
Taking a Quantum Leap *(L103)* Discovering Your Life Purpose *(L104)*
Balance, Stability, and Constancy *(L105)*
Becoming Self-Confident *(RE008)* Creating Your Perfect Day *(SI101)*
Meeting Your Spirit Guide (014) Opening Up Psychic Abilities (013)
Developing Intuition (010) Radiating Unconditional Love *(P103)*
Creating Money: Magnetizing Yourself *(SI010)*
Attracting Your Soul Mate *(RE002)*
Losing Weight, Looking Younger *(SI030)*
Getting in Touch with Your Power *(SI003)*
Being Your Higher Self *(SI040)*
Radiating Unconditional Love *(P103)*
Lucid Dreaming *(SI024)*
Reprogramming at a Cellular Level *(SI056)*
Overcoming the Self-Destruct *(SI060)* Clearing Blockages *(SI057)*
For the Self-Employed *(SI037)*
Public Recognition: Getting Your Work Out *(SI015)*
Many more single Orin journeys can be ordered on our website.

Transformation: Evolving Your Personality

These 8 Orin meditations assist you in handling blockages, doubts, mood swings, old issues coming up, over-stimulation, and things that come from being on an accelerated path of growth. Meditations include: *Self-Appreciation; Honoring Your Path of Awakening; Focusing Inward: Hearing Your Soul's Voice; Focusing Upward: Hearing the Voice of the Masters and Guides; Reparenting Yourself; Creating Your Future with Light; Beyond Intellect: Opening Your Higher Mind; and Journey to the Temple of the Masters to Reprogram at a Cellular Level.* (SG200)

Orin's Spiritual Vision Courses

Part 1, *Vision: Seeing and Sensing Subtle Energies.* Learn how to awaken your third eye to see and sense subtle energies, and to better see your higher purpose, what to manifest, and your path of spiritual growth. *(OR917)*

Part 2, *Vision: Creating Your Highest Future.* You will discover ways to see into time, to find those choices, decisions, and paths that create your highest future. *(OR918)*

Creating Money Audio Course

Creating Money: Attracting Abundance

To increase your prosperity consciousness, Orin has made these *Creating Money* guided meditations. These can assist you in reprogramming your subconscious to increase your abundance potential. The journeys in this series include: *Magnetizing Yourself (SI010) Clearing Beliefs and Old Programs (SI071) Releasing Doubts and Fears (SI075) Linking with Your Soul and the Guides (SI076) Aura Clearing, Energy and Lightwork (SI073) Awakening Your Prosperity Self (SI074) Success (SI070) Abundance (SI072)*. These can either be purchased separately or as a set. To order all 8 journeys, specify the album *(M100)*.

Creating Money Audio Book available on our website.

Orin's Becoming a World Server Course

Call upon those you can serve as a teacher, healer, leader, or in any capacity you choose. These meditations were given to Sanaya by Orin to assist her in getting Orin's work out to the world. Journeys include: *Discovering Your True Path; Sounding Your Note; Expanding Your Vision; Meeting Your Spiritual Community; Calling to You Those You Can Serve; Navigating the Flow; Being a Source of Light;* and *Becoming a World Server*. 8 meditations by Orin, music by Thaddeus. *(M200)* Also helpful: Public Recognition *(SI015)*

Orin's Living Your Life Purpose Course

Learn how to find and live your life purpose in every moment. View your life purpose as your higher self and soul and learn more about it. Learn how to call upon beings of light for strength and courage, and to empower you to find and live your life purpose in every moment. Receive energy from an Enlightened One to gain clarity and insight into the higher purpose of various areas of your life. Evolve your personality so that it can better carry out the goals of your higher self. Have greater clarity about what activities you are doing that are in alignment with your higher purpose, and release any that are not. 8 Orin journeys, music by Thaddeus. *(OR914)*

Orin's Becoming a Writer Audio Course

These powerful meditations contain the processes given to Sanaya by Orin to help get their books out to the world. Meditations include: **I Am a Writer, Manifesting Your Writing, Loving to Write, Connecting With Your Audience,** and processes to get your writing published. 4 meditations by Orin, music by Thaddeus. *(SI016)*

Opening to Channel
How to Connect With Your Guide
Revised Opening to Channel Audio Meditations
This audio course is a wonderful companion to the *Opening to Channel* book. It contains the processes taught by Sanaya and Duane at their Opening to Channel seminars with chapters on how to give readings from the *Opening to Channel* book, read by Sanaya. As you listen, Orin and DaBen join their energy with yours and lead you through each step of channeling, including relaxation, concentration, mentally meeting your guide, and learning to channel verbally. Processes include channeling state inductions to tune into another person, give yourself a reading, and see into the future. 25 programs include talks and guided journeys by Orin and DaBen. *(C101)* *(Replaces C100)*

Orin's *Channeling Your Guide:*
Receiving Clear Guidance
Work with your existing guide or meet a new guide to receive clear guidance that shows you how to create the divine perfection that is possible in every area of your life. This course is useful whether you have ever connected to a guide, or have worked with a guide for years. Receive clear guidance to create the highest possible future as you look into time, get more details, and see the bigger picture. Strengthen your connection to your guide and believe in the guidance you receive. Orin course, 12 journeys. *(C201)*

Orin's *Personal Power* Audio Courses
Part 1 Personal Power Through Awareness: Sensing Energy. Create the reality you want using energy, thought, and light. Develop your skills of visualizing. Sense the energy around you, increase your intuitive abilities, and receive higher guidance. Meditations include: *Sensing Energy; Sensing Unseen Energy; Sensing Energy in Others; Who Am I? Sensing Your Own Energy; Developing Intuition; Evolving Emotional Telepathy; Sending and Receiving Telepathic Images;* and *Receiving Higher Guidance.* 8 meditations *(P201)*

Part 2: Personal Power Through Awareness: Journey Into Light. Audio course by Orin. Experience yourself in new, higher ways, learn how to love yourself more, come from your power, stay in your center around others, and more. Meditations include: *Learning Unconditional Love; Handling Pain: Transforming Negative Energy; Bringing Your Unconscious Into Consciousness; Journey Into Light: Going Higher; Self-Love: Evolving Your Inner Dialogue; Transforming Your Inner Images; Finding Your Deepest Truth;* and *Wisdom: Being Your Higher Self.* 8 meditations *(P202)*

Spiritual Growth
Being Your Higher Self
Orin's Spiritual Growth Audio Meditations

Part 1: Spiritual Growth: Raising Your Vibration.
Guided meditations for: *Raising Your Vibration; Calming Your Emotions; Accelerating Your Spiritual Growth; Choosing Your Reality; Expanding and Contracting Time; Lifting the Veils of Illusion; Right Use of Will;* and *Becoming Transparent.* 8 meditations by Orin with music by Thaddeus. *(SG101)*

Part 2: Spiritual Growth: Being Your Higher Self.
Guided meditations for: *Being Your Higher Self; Creating With Light; Connecting With the Universal Mind; Linking With the Higher Will; Seeing the Bigger Picture; Opening Awareness of the Inner Planes; Allowing Your Higher Good;* and *Nonattachment.* 8 meditations by Orin with music by Thaddeus. *(SG102)*

Divine Self Courses:
Expand Into Your Innermost Self

Knowing Your True Identity. Open to know who you really are–a Self that has everything you need within you. When you realize what a vast consciousness you are, you no longer feel like a small, powerless, separate self. You gain more confidence and self-esteem. You are able to handle situations with greater wisdom, insight, and love. 12 Orin meditations *(DS201)*

Awakening Your Spiritual Power. Explore the truth that there is only one power, that of the Self within you. Discover what it means to live this truth as you open to the realization that nothing can have power over you, the true Self. 12 Orin meditations *(DS202)*

Clearing Energy with Your Divine Self. Open to the illumination of your Divine, innermost Self that clears any energy that veils your inner light, such as fears, emotions, beliefs, thoughts, and memories. You will discover how to stay in the clearest states possible, no matter what kind of energy you are around. When you are clear you feel good about yourself, you are more joyful, insightful, inspired, focused, confident, optimistic, and can follow your inner guidance to unfold your highest path. 20 Orin meditations *(DS203)*

Asking and Receiving from Your Divine Self. Orin created this course to assist you in opening to the infinite possibilities for good that await you in every area of your life. You no longer need to live with lack or limitation. Life need not be a struggle. You ask for so much less than you can have! Orin offers you these journeys to assist you in recognizing more of what you can ask for, in knowing that you can ask for and receive far more than you ever dreamed possible. 13 Orin meditations *(DS204)*

Soul Love Audio Meditations

Part 1 Soul Love—Awakening Your Heart Centers.
Experience more deeply the love, joy, and peace of your soul. As you listen, you will receive energy from Orin, the beings of light, and the World Teacher of Love. All these beings will join you to assist you in awakening your heart centers. Meditations include: *Making Soul Contact; Blending With Your Soul; Soul Linking; The Serenity of Love; The Oneness of Love; The Will to Love; Surrendering to Love;* and *Soul Love.* 8 meditations by Orin with beautiful music by Thaddeus. (*SL105*)

Part 2: Creating a Soul Relationship. Work soul-to-soul to transform a relationship. Increase the light and love between you and another at the soul level that can then manifest as powerful and wonderful changes in your daily life together. Also can be used to continue your connection to someone who has passed over, to link with them soul-to-soul. Meditations include: *Meeting Soul to Soul; Light Play; Love Play; Creating the Relationship You Want; Dissolving Obstacles to Love; Discovering New Ways to Love;* and *Soul Blending.* 8 meditations by Orin with beautiful music by Thaddeus. (*SL106*)

Orin's Millennium/Star Journeys
Expand Every Level of Your Being

The guided meditation audio courses by Orin that follow can assist you in accelerating your spiritual growth. Orin links you with Star energies from the Great Bear, Pleiades, Sirius, and the Spiritual Sun for transformation. These guided meditations can expand your consciousness, accelerate your evolution, and illuminate your mind. Each course contains 12 Orin journeys with music by Thaddeus.

Volume 1: Increasing Your Inner Light. Your inner light determines what you experience and draw to you. Increase your inner light to draw to you your higher good. (*MM010*)

Volume 2: Expanding Your Consciousness. Explore your higher purpose, receive energy from the beings of light, awaken your chakras, manifest your higher path, and more. (*MM020*)

Volume 3: Accelerating Your Evolution. Link with your soul and connect with the light of Spirit to accelerate your evolution. Experience soul vision; gain new insights and perspectives; transform your body, mind, and emotions to a higher vibration; express your inner truth. (*MM030*)

Volume 4: Building a Radiant Aura. Work with the angel of the devas – small angelic beings – to build a radiant aura. Your radiance determines the situations and circumstances of your life, and the type of energy you live in and around. You will purify your aura of negative energies, and create an aura filled with light. (*MM040*

Awakening Your Light Body: Keys to Enlightenment

A Six-Part Audio Course
by DaBen and Orin

Orin joins with DaBen to present *Awakening Your Light Body*, an audio course with extensive written material and 72 audio journeys in six parts to take you on a step-by-step spiritual growth program. This course is recommended for those of you who have been on a growth path for a while, and who want to experience many heightened, expanded states of consciousness, to take a quantum leap, and to increase your ability to sense the subtle energies of your soul and the soul plane. This course has created positive life changes and results beyond anything we imagined for ourselves and others.

What Is Your Light Body?

Many of you are in the process of making the evolutionary leap of awakening your light bodies. Your light body is an energy body that exists at a higher level, closer to your soul, than your chakras.

As you awaken your lower energy body centers, you can regulate the amount of energy you take in from your environment, change less harmonious energies into higher ones, and use the energy around you to go higher. As you awaken these centers, you may experience a stronger sense of personal power and a greater ability to control your emotions, stay centered, release old blocks and stuck emotional energy, and respond with love.

Your upper centers open doorways to the higher realms of light, such as the soul plane. Awakening them assists you in adding light to your thoughts, opening your channel upward, and connecting with the Universal Mind. There are three light body centers besides the lower and upper energy body centers. As you awaken these centers, you become a radiating source of light. You can more easily choose those actions that reflect the light of your soul and higher self. You can experience many illumined states of awareness. These states of consciousness can feel deeply insightful, blissful, and take you beyond thought into direct experiences of beingness. You will be able to see, sense, or feel the expanded, more beautiful energies of the higher dimensions and make them a part of your life.

Are You Ready to Awaken Your Light Body?

Visit our website at www.orindaben.com and take a fun quiz to determine if you are ready to awaken your light body.

Divine Will Audio Courses

Align with the 7 qualities of Divine Will to transform your life. As you align with Divine Will, you infuse your personality with new skills and more power to carry out your soul's higher goals and purposes. Working in this way can release blockages and limitations and create profound and wonderful changes.

Transforming Your Life with Divine Will

To align with Divine Will you need to contact it, call it to you, and draw it into your life. Work with seven qualities of Divine Will to transform your life, unfold your potential, expand your consciousness, open your spiritual vision, deepen your intuition, release limitations, and enable you to create your highest future. 12 audio meditations by Orin and extensive written material. (MM050)

Living a Soul Life with Divine Will

Link with the seven qualities of Divine Will to awaken to divine love, strengthen self-love, transform your emotions, illuminate your mind, know your life purpose, increase abundance and prosperity, receive clear inner guidance, expand your creativity, evolve your body, create a supportive environment, and live your life as a soul. 12 audio meditations by Orin, extensive written material. (MM060)

Transforming Your Consciousness:
Clearing Lesser Energies, Illusions, and Limitations

Work with a quality of Divine Will that allows you to release the thoughts, illusions, lesser energies, and obstacles that stand in the way of living as your soul–free, joyous, clear, loving, peaceful, and harmonious. Release lower, denser energies, thoughts, emotions, desires, and the fogs of illusions. 10 Orin journeys, written material. (DW911)

Experiencing Continuity of Consciousness:
Discovering Your Soul's Path

Connect with the second quality of Divine Will to learn much more about the essence of your being and the skills, purposes, and directions that have appeared throughout your lifetimes on earth. Expand your awareness of who you are, and know more about why you are here and what you are here to do. 6 Orin journeys, talks by Sanaya, and written material. (DW912)

Evolving Your Consciousness:
Stepping Onto Your Highest Path

Link with your soul and a third quality of Divine Will called the Will to Evolve to find and to step onto your highest path. Play in the infinite potential of the Universal Mind where you will meet your future enlightened Self. This Self will light up your highest path, a path that leads to enlightenment in the most effective, direct way; that accelerates your evolution, and that assists you to manifest your highest potential in this lifetime. 9 Orin journeys. (DW913)

Intuition: Connecting With Your Divine Self

Link with your soul and the fourth quality of Divine Will, the Will to Harmonize. Orin guides you to open all channels of communication to your Divine Self, the source of intuitive guidance. Through this connection, you can awaken your clairvoyance and clairaudience, and clear emotions and thoughts that stand in the way of your receiving, hearing, and correctly interpreting your intuition. 10 Orin journeys. (DW914)

Illumination: Awakening Your Higher Mind

Link with the fifth quality of Divine Will to release thoughts and beliefs that create disease, pain, suffering, lack, limitation, doubt, disharmony, blockages, or discord in any area of your life. Have thoughts that lead to your liberation and enlightenment. Link your mind with your higher mind and the Universal Mind to experience unlimited abundance, joy, harmony, good health, loving relationships, and peace. 10 Orin journeys. (DW915)

Inspiration: Being Your Authentic Self

Link with the sixth quality of Divine Will so that all you do brings you peace and joy, rather than pain or suffering. Be your true Self, speak your truth, transform your relationships, change the roles you play, and experience more love, vision, freedom, purity, perfection, inner stillness, balance, one-pointedness, endurance, fearlessness, and patience. 19 Orin journeys. (DW916)

Divine Manifesting with the
Seven Qualities of Divine Will

Part 1: Manifesting as Your Divine Self (MM070)
Part 2 Becoming a Master of Manifesting (DW918)

This is Orin's most advanced and transformative courses on manifesting, and it has created profound results for people who have taken it. Call upon seven Great Ones who radiate Divine Will to better connect with your Divine Self, and to experience the power, love, harmony, wisdom, illumination, intuition, and inspiration of your Divine Self. With this connection you can more perfectly create the Divine blueprint in every area of your life. When you manifest as your Divine Self, you draw to you situations, forms, relationships, and circumstances that bring you joy, peace, harmony, abundance, love, and all good things. People have had astounding results not only in manifesting outer things but also in transforming their consciousness as they worked with both Parts 1 and 2 of Orin's *Divine Manifesting* course.

Transcending Your Ego Audio Courses

Orin's journeys in this series are uplifting and expansive, guiding you to experience the illumination of the Divine Self that reveals your ego and the ways your ego has limited you or caused you to suffer. You can then use your increased illumination to change for the better your thoughts, emotions, and daily life. All albums in this series contain 12 guided meditations by Orin.

Volume 1: Birthing a New You

Are you ready to experience your life and consciousness in new ways, to know more joy, love, peace, harmonious relationships, and abundance? Are you ready to know the magnificence of your Divine Self as who you are? Includes: • *Opening to Your Divine Self* • *Awakening Your Spiritual Power* *Trusting Your Inner Wisdom* • *Calling Upon Divine Self Inspiration* • *Transforming Limiting Thoughts* • *Experiencing More Freedom in Your Life* • *Tapping Into Infinite Supply* • *Receiving Divine Self Guidance* • *Knowing the Peace of Your Divine Self* • *Rising Into Divine Consciousness* • *Enjoying Harmonious Relationships* • *Birthing a New You*. (DS101)

Volume 2: Transforming Your Emotions

Connect with your Divine Self to release negative emotions. As the fogs of strong emotions dissipate in the light of your Divine Self, a path opens up into many higher states of consciousness that are only possible to experience with flowing and peaceful emotions. Includes: • *Awakening Divine Love* • *Staying Clear Around Negative Emotions* • *Creating Positive Emotions About Your Body* • *Changing a Situation by Freeing Stuck Emotions* • *Dissolving Blockages to Divine Self Contact* • *Clearing Obstacles to Experiencing Infinite Supply* • *Choosing the Rewards of a Peaceful Life* • *Loving Yourself by Refusing Negative Emotions* • *Freeing Yourself From Repeating the Past* • *Releasing Pain* • *Deepening and Sustaining Inner Peace* • *Accepting More Peace, Joy, and Love*. (DS102)

Volume 3: Evolving Your Desire Body

Evolve your desire body so that it responds to Divine Will and to your Divine Self rather than to mass consciousness or other people's desires. Create circumstances that fulfill you. Experience yourself as radiant light, love, and wisdom. Includes: • *Increasing Your Desire for Divine Self Contact* • *Reorienting Your Desire Body* • *Aligning Your Desires With Higher Purpose* • *Freeing Yourself From Unfulfilling Desires* • *Becoming Pure Awareness Without Desire* • *Evolving Your Desire Body* • *Exploring Your New Desire Body* • *Releasing Past Desires* • *Opening to the Opportunity in Each Moment* • *Accelerating Your Transformation* • *Elevating All the Energies About You* • *Living an Inspired Life*. (DS103)

Volume 4: Illuminating Your Mind

Experience pure awareness–states of stillness where you can receive creative thoughts and clear inner guidance. Then your thoughts show you the way and bring you peace and solutions. Includes: • *Experiencing the Light That Reveals the Mind* • *Realizing the True Nature of Thoughts* • *Rising Above Mind–Chatter* • *Responding to Your Thoughts in New Ways* • *Letting Go of Worry Thoughts* • *Freeing Yourself From Limiting Beliefs* • *Dissolving Fixed Opinions: Awakening Divine Vision* • *Strengthening Divine Self Guidance* • *Connecting With the Divine Self of Others* • *Receiving Divine Ideas: Opening to New Possibilities* • *Releasing Limiting Thoughts About Your Body and Aging* • *Illuminating Your Mind*. (DS104)

Volume 5: Deepening Divine Self Consciousness

Experience the great, revealing, illuminating light of your Divine Self. This illumination makes it possible to transcend your ego in even more profound, life-changing ways. The sun of the Self radiates Its light into your mind, desires, and emotions, into anywhere you have been closed, limited, or stuck. It frees you! Includes: • *Breaking Through to New Consciousness* • *Becoming Pure Awareness Without Thoughts* • *Coming into Resonance With Your Divine Self* • *Experiencing a New You: Letting Go of Old Identities* • *Updating the Roles You Play* • *Asking and Receiving From Your Divine Self* • *Knowing Your Formless Self* • *Freeing Yourself From Past Labels* • *Into the Light: Clearing the Storms of Emotions* • *Being True to Your Self* • *Recognizing the Divine in Others* • *Embracing Your New Identity*. (DS105)

Volume 6: Transcending Your Ego

Experience many wonderful states of illumination where lesser thoughts and desires release themselves from you. Emotions become more balanced, flowing, and peaceful. Experience what a gift it is, what joy, when the clouds of the ego part and the light of your Divine Self bursts forth from within you. There is a feeling of well-being, as if you are lifting out of the darkness into the light of day. Includes: • *Stabilizing Your Emotions* • *Experiencing Desirelessness* • *Receiving Gifts of Consciousness* • *Rising Above Your Ego* • *Freeing Yourself From Attachments* • *Practicing Self–Forgiveness* • *Releasing the Need to Suffer* • *Moving Beyond Needing Approval* • *Letting Things Be* • *Responding As Your Divine Self* • *Allowing a New Consciousness to Arise* • *Radiating Your Inner Beauty*. (DS106)

As you open to your Divine Self you have access to all the consciousness, love, wisdom, and unlimited abundance that your Divine Self has to offer, which is freely and gladly given.

Free on our Website at
www.orindaben.com

Come visit our website and enjoy connecting with us. You can have fun in various ways:

• **Read** more about Orin and Sanaya Roman.

• Click on the *Living with Joy* book cover in the *Creating Your Highest Future* room and receive uplifting quotes from the book, and from any of our books.

• **Sign our guestbook** and **receive our eNewsletter** containing up to date information from Orin, free audio meditations, and more. Let us know about you; we love hearing from you.

• Receive a free Orin printed **newsletter.**

• Read **articles by Orin** on many spiritual topics.

• Read **weekly meditations and weekly book excerpts.**

• Listen to **free short online Orin meditations** on topics such as self-love, clearing blockages, clear and creative thinking, receiving solar light, increasing soul vision, making soul contact, receiving abundance, relaxation, feeling energized, loving relationships, radiating unconditional love, cellular activation, and more.

• Listen to free full-length Orin meditations to assist you in transforming your life and consciousness.

• Get **personal daily affirmations** on health, creating money and abundance, loving relationships, losing weight, health and well-being, clearing blockages, increasing psychic abilities and intuition, opening your channel, loving yourself, and more.

• Sanaya brings through angelic music through a being named Thaddeus. You can **listen to Thaddeus' music online.**

Free Orin Newsletters and eNewsletters

Visit our website and subscribe to our free newsletter containing articles and affirmations, and information about Orin's audio courses and books. We offer "eNewsletters" sent to you several times a year (not the same as our printed newsletter) if we have your email address. These contain links to free Orin audio meditations and articles. These are Orin's way of continuing to assist you in living with joy by providing you with information, processes, and his transmissions of energy. We have many free offerings on our website; see last page of this book for more information.